HOLT
1
SPANISH

¡Ven conmigo!®

Video Guide

HOLT, RINEHART AND WINSTON

A Harcourt Classroom Education Company

Austin · New York · Orlando · Atlanta · San Francisco · Boston · Dallas · Toronto · London

Contributing Writers:

Mary Atkinson

Eleanor Hardin

Jan Underwood

Reviewers:

Richard Lindley

Mayanne Wright

Cover Photo Credits:

Group of students: Marty Granger/HRW Photo; videocassette: Image Copyright ©2003 Photodisc, Inc.

Photo Credits:

All photos by Marty Granger/Edge Video Productions/HRW except:

Page 4, (br) Josef Beck/FPG International, (bc) SuperStock, (br) Steve Vidler/Leo de Wys, (b) D. Murray/Edge Productions/HRW; 18, (bl) G. Gscheidle/Image Bank, (bc) Tom Owen Edmunds/Image Bank, (bc) SuperStock; 32, (br) SuperStock; 36, (viento) Michelle Bridwell/Frontera Fotos, (lluvia) King/H. Armstrong Roberts, (nieve) Randy O'Rourke/The Stock Market; 43, Lisa Davis; 46, (bc) Suzanne L. Murphy/DDB Stock; 56, (r) Sam Dudgeon/HRW; 60, (bc) Michael Salas/Image Bank; 74, (br) Ira Block/Image Bank; 78, (l) Michael Newman/Photo Edit, (r) Michelle Bridwell/HRW Photo; 84, (tl) Dan Morrison Photography, (tr) David R. Frazier Photolibrary

Printed in the United States of America

ISBN 0-03-065904-3

1 2 3 4 5 6 7   066   05 04 03 02 01

To the Teacher

The *¡Ven conmigo!*® *Video Program* was shot entirely on location in Spanish-speaking regions and supplies linguistically authentic and culturally rich video support for your classroom.

The *Video Program* is available in two formats, on standard videocassette and on DVD. Using the *DVD Tutor* and a DVD video player to show the video allows you to quickly and easily access any segment of the video program and to repeat small segments instantly and as often as needed. The *DVD Tutor* also provides video-based activities to assess student comprehension and allows you to display still images from any part of the program. Video material for chapters 1-6 is contained on Disc 1; material for chapters 7-12 is on Disc 2. *

The *Video Program* provides the following video support for each chapter of the *Pupil's Edition*:

- A narrated **Location Opener** gives students a guided tour to the geography, culture, and people of each of the six regions explored in the *Pupil's Edition*.

- The **De antemano** section of each chapter is enacted on video. The scripted, controlled language supported by visual cues provides comprehensible input that models the targeted functional expressions, vocabulary, and grammar. This section can be used to present material in the chapter for the first time, to reinforce it as you go through the chapter, and to review it at the end of a lesson cycle.

- The stories presented in **De antemano** are continued and bring closure to the dramatic episodes. Look for the sections that contain the episode title and **(a continuación)**. This expanded story allows for additional modeling of targeted functions, vocabulary, and grammar, as well as recycling and spiraling of previously learned material.

- Spanish captions for every **De antemano** and **a continuación** are available on Videocassette 5. Target-language captions give students another opportunity to comprehend the language in the story and offer teachers further possibilities for presenting the new material in class.

- The **Panorama cultural** section presents videotaped interviews with the native speakers of Spanish introduced on the **Panorama cultural** page in the *Pupil's Edition* as well as additional interviews with several other people from around the Spanish-speaking world. The unscripted language spoken at a normal rate of speed will give students a taste of "real" Spanish. Teaching suggestions and activity masters in this guide will help students focus on the pertinent information and make the language accessible to them.

- A special **Videoclips** section provides authentic television footage related to the chapter theme including commercials, weather reports, and music videos. These authentic Spanish-language television clips give students an opportunity to hear and enjoy material produced for native speakers of Spanish and not specifically designed for language learners. In order to preserve authenticity, this material was not edited for the classroom and should be previewed by teachers to ensure compliance with local guidelines.

- **Colorín colorado** provides further practice with the chapter's functional expressions and vocabulary, and is designed to be done after students have completed the chapter in the *Pupil's Edition*.

This *Video Guide* provides background information and suggestions for pre-viewing, viewing, and post-viewing activities for all portions of the *Video Program*. It also contains scripts and synopses for all dramatic episodes, transcripts of all interviews and **Videoclips,** supplementary vocabulary lists, and reproducible activity masters for use with all sections of the program.

---

*In addition to the video material and the video-based comprehension activities, the *DVD Tutor* also contains the entire *Interactive CD-ROM Tutor* in DVD-ROM format. Each DVD disc contains the activities from all 1 2 chapters of the *Interactive CD-ROM Tutor*. This part of the *DVD Tutor* may be used on any Macintosh® or Windows® computer with a DVD-ROM drive.

Contents

 The DVD Tutor contains all video material. Chapters 1-6 are on Disc 1 and Chapters 7-12 are on Disc 2.

CAPÍTULO PRELIMINAR

¡Adelante!

DVD Tutor, Disc 1
Videocassette 1
Start Time: 1:15
Length: 3:15
Pupil's Edition pp. xxx–11

You may wish to play the video for the **Capítulo preliminar** as a preview to the program and as an introduction to the Spanish language. In the video, people from various Spanish-speaking countries introduce themselves. Two young girls recite the Spanish alphabet, and a small boy counts from one to eleven.

 Teaching Suggestions

 The Preliminary Chapter of the Video Program is also available on the DVD Tutor, Disc 1.

Pre-viewing

- Hold a class discussion about where major languages of the world are spoken. Have students brainstorm and make a list of Spanish-speaking regions and countries. Write the list on the board or on a transparency. Have students locate them on a globe or on the world map found on pp. xxiv–xxv of the *Pupil's Edition*.

- Ask students how they think people in Spanish-speaking regions look and dress. Point out that people in most countries dress differently depending on whether they live in the city or in the country.

Viewing

- Show the video without sound and ask students what they think the hand gestures that are used mean. (Welcome!, Hi!, Come with me!) Then show the video with sound and have students listen for the corresponding expressions in Spanish. (**¡Bienvenidos!, ¡Hola!, ¡Ven conmigo!**)

- Have students write the names of the three countries they are welcomed to at the beginning of the video. (Costa Rica, Venezuela, Argentina) Also have students write the number of Spanish-speaking people in the world (almost 350 million), and in the United States (over 20 million) as mentioned in the video.

- Replay the segment featuring the map without sound. Have students name the countries and regions as they are highlighted. Point out the areas students will visit in the 12 chapters of the video: Spain, Mexico, Florida, Ecuador, Texas, and Puerto Rico.

- Tell students to listen to how the people being interviewed pronounce their names. You may want to pause after each person speaks and have students as a class or individually repeat the name aloud. Then, ask students how these pronunciations differ from the corresponding English pronunciation. Have students listen for sounds that English doesn't have. (**r, rr**)

- Have students listen to the girls say the alphabet and see if they can pick out the letter that they leave out. (the letter **n**) Point out the similarity between the **n** and **ñ** as a possible reason for this mistake. You may also want to point out that the girls are from Costa Rica and say **uve**, **doble uve**, and **ye** for **u, w,** and **y**. Other Spanish speakers may say **ve, doble ve,** and **i griega**.

Post-viewing

- Discuss how students' impressions of Spanish-speaking people have changed after watching the video. Write a list of students' comments on a transparency or on the board.

- Complete the list of Spanish-speaking countries that students began before viewing the video.

- Individually or in pairs, students may use what they learned in the video to calculate what percentage of the world's population speaks Spanish and what percentage of the United States does. (about six percent of the world population and eight percent of the U.S. population)

Activity Master 1

Viewing

1. Match the name of each person in the video with his or her picture.

   a. Ilda de Betencourt   **c.** Johnny José Martínez
   b. Jennifer   **d.** Yamilé Anthony

   1. _____   2. _____   3. _____   4. _____

2. Put the following numbers in the order in which Robi says them.

   _____ tres   _____ cinco   _____ seis

   _____ ocho   _____ siete   _____ cuatro

   _____ diez   _____ dos   _____ once

   _____ uno   _____ nueve

Post-viewing

3. Circle the continents where Spanish is spoken.

   Africa   Europe

   Antarctica   North America

   Asia   South America

   Australia

CAPÍTULO PRELIMINAR

Location Opener for Chapters 1-2

Location: España

DVD Tutor, Disc 1
Videocassette 1
Start Time: 4:31
Length: 2:15
Pupil's Edition pp. 12–15

The Spanish in the Location Opener is spoken at a normal speed. Students are not expected to understand everything. The activities for this section have been designed to help them understand the major points.

 Teaching Suggestions

 The DVD Tutor contains all video material plus a video-based activity to assess student comprehension after viewing the Location Opener. Short segments are automatically replayed to prompt students if they answer incorrectly.

Pre-viewing

- Ask students what they already know about Spain and what they might expect to see on the video. List their responses on a transparency or on the board. Keep the list handy for follow-up.

- Ask students to locate **Madrid, Barcelona, Pamplona, los Pirineos, Sevilla,** and **Valencia** on the map on p. xxiii of the *Pupil's Edition*.

Viewing

- Show the video without sound. Have students write a list of what they see in the video (for instance, castles, skiing, windsurfing, windmills).

- While showing the video without sound, pause at different locations and give students background information of some of the places shown. For example, explain to students that many cities in Spanish-speaking countries have a central square called the **plaza mayor**. In Madrid, **la Plaza Mayor** is a popular meeting place. Located in the center of the square is a statue of Felipe III. You may want to point out that a **tuna** is a group of strolling musicians made up of university students who follow a centuries-old tradition of dressing in traditional costume and playing music. Another point of interest is the **fallas**, a popular Valencian celebration that takes place in March. During this celebration, elaborate floats are paraded and then burned at the end of the week. Another celebration that is featured in the Location Opener is the **festival de San Fermín,** or **los Sanfermines**. It is better known in the United States as the "Running of the Bulls," made famous by Ernest Hemingway's novel *The Sun Also Rises*.

- Show the video with sound. Ask students to complete Activities 1, 2, and 3 on Activity Master, p. 4. You may want to show the video more than once.

Post-viewing

- Ask questions about the different locations in the video. For example: Where do the **fallas** take place? (Valencia) In what city do the Spanish celebrate **los Sanfermines**? (Pamplona)

- The video presents many opportunities for launching in-depth research reports about any of the cultural traditions, geographical areas, or varied architectural styles of Spain. You may want to ask students to pick one aspect of the video and work in groups or pairs to find out more about Spain.

- Review the students' list of expectations about Spain prepared as a Pre-viewing activity suggestion. Have them compare the list with their lists made while viewing the video. Ask students if the video confirmed their expectations or modified them. Ask them how else they might test their preconceptions. (invite a guest speaker who has been to Spain; research a topic in the library; consult the cultural sections in their textbook)

Activity Master: Location Opener

Supplementary Vocabulary

la arquitectura *architecture*	esquiar *to ski*
la ciudad cosmopolita *cosmopolitan city*	las fallas de Valencia *a spring celebration*
la costa *coast*	la montaña *mountain*
en el norte *in the north*	la playa *beach*
en el sur *in the south*	la tabla vela *wind surfing*

Viewing

1. Place a check mark next to each phrase as you hear it in the video.

   _____ **a.** las montañas nevadas   _____ **e.** Madrid, capital de España

   _____ **b.** las playas blancas   _____ **f.** la arquitectura inimitable de Gaudí

   _____ **c.** un país de muchas costas   _____ **g.** Sevilla, con toda su elegancia

   _____ **d.** las fiestas de los Sanfermines   _____ **h.** los diversos paisajes de España

2. Match each Spanish city with what it's famous for.

   _____ 1. Valencia   a. museos, palacios y tiendas

   _____ 2. Pamplona   b. ciudad preciosa en el sur de España

   _____ 3. Madrid   c. los Sanfermines

   _____ 4. Barcelona   d. Gaudí

   _____ 5. Sevilla   e. las fallas

Post-viewing

3. Match each picture with the phrase that best describes it.

   a. España es un país de muchas costas.

   b. La arquitectura de Gaudí distingue a Barcelona.

   c. Sevilla es una ciudad preciosa de Andalucía.

   d. En el norte se puede esquiar en los Pirineos.

1. _____   2. _____   3. _____   4. _____

¡Mucho gusto!

Functions modeled in video:

- saying hello and goodbye
- introducing people and responding to an introduction
- asking how someone is and saying how you are
- asking and saying how old someone is
- asking where someone is from and saying where you're from
- talking about likes and dislikes

DVD 1 The DVD Tutor provides instant access to any part of the video program as well as the ability to repeat short segments as needed. The DVD Tutor also allows access to Spanish-language captions for all video segments as well as to video-based comprehension activities to assess student comprehension.

Video Segment	Correlation to Print Materials			Videocassette 1		Videocassette 5 (captioned)	
	Pupil's Edition	Video Guide		Start Time	Length	Start Time	Length
		Activity Masters	Scripts				
De antemano	pp. 18–19	p. 8	p. 88	7:07	4:03	0:00:50	4:04
A continuación		p. 9	p. 88	11:11	5:14	0:04:53	5:17
Panorama cultural	p. 31*	p. 10	p. 89	16:26	2:05		
Videoclips		p. 10	p. 89	18:31	4:31		

Video Synopses

De antemano ¡Me llamo Francisco!

Paco is hoping that Ramón, the mail carrier, is going to bring a letter from his new pen pal. Ramón pretends not to have a letter for Paco because the letter is addressed to "Francisco," Paco's full name. While Paco is reading the letter and daydreaming about his pen pal, his friend Felipe stops by for a visit.

¡Me llamo Francisco! (a continuación)

Paco and Felipe go to meet Mercedes, Paco's pen pal. She arrives at the pizzeria with her friend Juanita. Paco and Mercedes know each other from school as Paco and Merche. After some awkward moments, they realize that they are one another's pen pal, but under their full names Francisco and Mercedes.

Panorama cultural ¿De dónde eres?

- Students from Puerto Rico, Spain, Costa Rica, and Venezuela tell where they are from.
- In additional interviews, people from various parts of the Spanish-speaking world tell us where they are from.

Videoclips

Colombia: promotional piece directed by Edgar González

The DVD Tutor contains all video material plus video-based activities to assess student comprehension of **De antemano, A continuación,** and **Panorama cultural.** Short video segments are automatically replayed to prompt students if they answer incorrectly.

De antemano ¡Me llamo Francisco!

Pre-viewing

Ask students if they have ever had a pen pal. Have them brainstorm as a class and make a list of the kinds of things they would want to know about a pen pal. Then, have them work in groups of three and list specific details that they would want to tell their pen pals about themselves.

Viewing

- Show the video without sound. Ask students to jot down notes on the similarities and differences they observe between Madrid and where they live. At the end of the segment, have students share and discuss their lists. You may want to make special note of the fact that Paco lives in an apartment above the **frutería**, his parents' business.

- Show the video with sound. Ask students to complete Activities 2 and 3 on Activity Master 1, p. 8. You may want to show the video more than once.

Post-viewing

- Ask students how many last names Paco and Mercedes each have. Refer to the **Nota cultural** on p. 20 of the *Pupil's Edition* to discuss how Spaniards and Latin Americans commonly have two last names. Have some of the students tell the class what their full name would be if they were living in a Spanish-speaking country.

- Ask students to compare the young people in the video with young people in their school. Ask if they think it would be a big adjustment to live in Madrid. Why or why not?

¡Me llamo Francisco! (a continuación)

Pre-viewing

Discuss with students how first names are often shortened in English, among friends, or in informal settings. Point out examples like *Jim* for *James*, or *Pat* for *Patricia*. Have students make a brief list of the people they know who go by the shortened version of their names. Then, point out the shortened versions of the Spanish names on p. 5 of the *Pupil's Edition*.

Viewing

Have students list the words that Paco uses to describe himself. Ask students if they think Paco's description of himself is accurate.

Post-viewing

- Ask students if they think it is possible to get an accurate picture of what another person is like through a letter. Why or why not? Discuss the different impressions the characters may have had of each other before meeting.

- Ask students to compare the way people in the video introduce and greet each other with the way they would do so. You may wish to ask students who are native speakers to tell about special ways of introducing or greeting people in their family or community.

Panorama cultural

Pre-viewing
- Ask students what would be the first two or three things they would tell about themselves when meeting someone from another place.
- Take a survey in your class to determine how many students are from somewhere other than the city they are living in now. Ask these students in Spanish where they are from. List all of the different places that are represented in your class. You may want to post maps of the United States or the world around the room and have students attach self-stick notes with their names on them beside their birth place.

Viewing
- You may want to show the video more than once. The first time through, students should write a list with the name of each person interviewed and where each is from. Then, have students watch the interviews and complete Activity 1 on Activity Master 3, p. 10.
- The first **Panorama cultural** activity on Activity Master 3 is based on the first four interviews only.
- Ask students if they can figure out why Jacó is embarrassed and laughing. (he was about to say he's sixteen, not seventeen)
- Have students write down the names of the interviewees who only mention the city they are from. Then ask students if they would mention their state and country when telling someone from another country where they are from.
- Point out that Eduardo says he's from **el Distrito Federal** although the caption says **México**. Tell students that **Distrito Federal** is Mexico City and is abbreviated **D.F.** Make the comparison between the capital of Mexico (**Distrito Federal**) and the capital of the United States. (District of Columbia)

Post-viewing
Ask students to locate where the interviewees live by pointing to the countries on the map on pp. xxiv–xxv of the *Pupil's Edition*.

Videoclips

- Have students locate Colombia on the map on p. xxvii of the *Pupil's Edition*.
- Have students try to determine how many times the name **Colombia** is heard in the song. (six) Show the videoclip as many times as needed for them to do this successfully.
- Ask students what the purpose of the videoclip is. (to encourage pride in Colombia) Ask students whether the videoclip has succeeded in doing this, and why.
- Mention that the children are shown dancing the **cumbia**, Colombia's most popular rhythm.

Colorín colorado *(It's a wrap)*

Have students conduct interviews similar to the ones in the **Panorama cultural**. Students can work in pairs to ask each other in Spanish where they're from.

Activity Master 1

CAPÍTULO 1

De antemano *¡Me llamo Francisco!*

Supplementary Vocabulary		
cuéntame *tell me*	está aquí *...is here*	Oye *Hey*
¿De quién? *From whom?*	fenomenal *great*	¿Qué es eso? *What's that?*

Pre-viewing

1. If you were to write to a pen pal, you might want to tell him or her what you are like. Look at the list of adjectives below and underline the ones that best describe you.

cómico/a   impaciente   nervioso/a   popular

emocional   inteligente   organizado/a   sentimental

fantástico/a   interesante   paciente   sincero/a

Viewing

2. Match the video characters with the phrases they say.

1. _____   2. _____   3. _____   4. _____

a. Tú no te llamas Francisco. Tú te llamas Paco.   **c.** ¡Lo siento, mamá!

b. Me gusta la pizza y me gusta mucho el voleibol...   **d.** Oye, está aquí tu amigo Felipe.

3. Put the following phrases in the order in which they are said.

_____ **a.** ¡Soy yo! Yo soy Francisco.   _____ **c.** Muy bien, gracias. ¿Y tú?

_____ **b.** ¿Cuántos años tienes?   _____ **d.** Paco, soy tu amigo.

Post-viewing

4. Which of the following statements best describes what happened in the video?

_____ **a.** Paco receives a letter from his friend Felipe.

_____ **b.** The mailman doesn't have a letter for Paco.

_____ **c.** Paco receives a letter from a girl named Mercedes.

_____ **d.** Paco receives a postcard from his pen pal in the United States.

Activity Master 2

¡Me llamo Francisco! (a continuación)

Viewing

Supplementary Vocabulary	
alto/a *tall*	organizado/a *organized*
guapo/a *good-looking*	el sábado *Saturday*
inteligente *intelligent*	sincero/a *sincere*
¿Me ayudas? *Will you help me?*	Tengo una cita. *I have a date.*

1. Place a check mark next to those items that Paco says he likes.

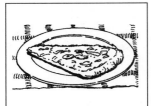 a. _____

 d. _____

 b. _____

 e. _____

 c. _____

 f. _____

2. What name is Merche short for?_____

3. What name is Paco short for?_____

Post-viewing

4. Write a list of the adjectives Paco uses to describe himself.

_____   _____   _____

_____   _____

5. Get together in groups of three or four and discuss whether or not Paco exaggerates a little in his description of himself. Make a list of some adjectives that would better describe Paco. You may want to look at the list of adjectives on Activity Master 1, p. 8.

_____   _____   _____

_____   _____   _____

Activity Master 3

Panorama cultural

Viewing

1. Draw a line matching the name of the person to the place he or she is from.

Ivette

Sandra

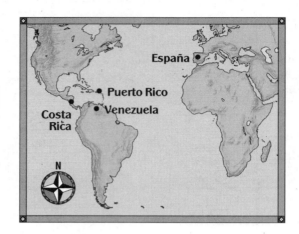

Mauricio

Miguel

2. Match each person with the place he or she is from.

_____ 1. Manolo   **a.** Colombia

_____ 2. Alexis   **b.** California

_____ 3. Eric   **c.** Texas

_____ 4. María Luisa   **d.** Puerto Rico

_____ 5. Aurora   **e.** Ecuador

Videoclips

Viewing

3. Listen carefully for the refrain, "**Cantando, cantando, yo viviré / Colombia, tierra querida.**"

How many times is it repeated in the song? _____

> **Supplementary Vocabulary**
> cantando *singing*
> tierra querida *beloved land*
> yo viviré *I'll live*

Post-viewing

4. List five similarities and five differences between Colombia and the place where you live. Write the similarities in the column on the left and the differences in the column on the right. Compare your lists with a classmate's.

Semejanzas	Diferencias
_____	_____
_____	_____
_____	_____
_____	_____
_____	_____

CAPÍTULO 1

CAPÍTULO

2

¡Organízate!

Functions modeled in video:

 DVD 1 The DVD Tutor provides instant access to any part of the video program as well as the ability to repeat short segments as needed. The DVD Tutor also allows access to Spanish-language captions for all video segments as well as to video-based comprehension activities to assess student comprehension.

- talking about what you want and need
- describing the contents of your room
- talking about what you need and want to do

Video Segment	Correlation to Print Materials			Videocassette 1		Videocassette 5 (captioned)	
	Pupil's Edition	Video Guide		Start Time	Length	Start Time	Length
		Activity Masters	Scripts				
De antemano	pp. 48–49	p. 14	p. 90	23:18	4:58	0:10:12	4:56
A continuación		p. 15	p. 90	28:18	6:50	0:15:09	6:54
Panorama cultural	p. 55*	p. 16	p. 91	35:38	3:59		
Videoclips		p. 16	p. 91	39:38	0:40		

 Video Synopses

De antemano ¡Mañana es el primer día de clases!

Paco explains to his grandmother that he needs to buy school supplies. His grandmother gives him money to buy what he needs but tells him that he has to clean his room first. Paco tries to clean his room quickly by throwing everything in his desk drawer and under his bed. When he finishes, he realizes he has lost the money his grandmother gave him.

¡Mañana es el primer día de clases! (a continuación)

Paco begins to tear apart his room looking for the lost money. His grandmother comes in and is shocked at the mess. While helping him look for the money, his grandmother realizes that Paco already has most of the school supplies he thought he needed. After finding the money, Paco and his friend Felipe go shopping for the things he still needs for school.

Panorama cultural ¿Qué necesitas para el colegio?

- Students from Ecuador, Venezuela, and Argentina tell us what they need to buy before the school year starts.
- In additional interviews, students from various Spanish-speaking countries tell us about what they need to buy for school.

Videoclips

Alfabetismo: public service message about illiteracy

Spanish 1 ¡Ven conmigo!

CAPÍTULO 2

Video Guide **11**

Teaching Suggestions

The DVD Tutor contains all video material plus video-based activities to assess student comprehension of **De antemano, A continuación,** and **Panorama cultural.** Short video segments are automatically replayed to prompt students if they answer incorrectly.

De antemano ¡Mañana es el primer día de clases!

Pre-viewing

Ask students what they do to get ready for the first day of school every year. Have students brainstorm and make a list in English of the items they need for school.

Viewing

- Point out to students that Paco's grandmother lives with him and his family. Tell students that many Spanish families maintain strong ties with the extended family, and three generations will often live in the same home.

- As students watch the video, have them listen for the school supplies that Paco says he needs. Ask them which two items on Paco's list are not considered school supplies. (**estéreo, pósters**)

- Ask students what kind of CD Paco's grandmother is listening to. (**zarzuela**) Explain that **zarzuela** is a traditional Spanish musical art form similar to short comic opera.

Post-viewing

Ask students to work in small groups or pairs to discuss how Paco's list of what he needs for school differs from before he cleans his room to after he cleans his room. Have students write a list of what he needs before cleaning it and a list of what he needs afterwards.

¡Mañana es el primer día de clases! (a continuación)

Pre-viewing

- Ask a volunteer to summarize the events in **De antemano**. Why does Paco clean his room? What is Paco's problem at the end? Have students discuss where they think the money is.

- Ask students what they usually say when they answer the telephone and talk to friends.

- Discuss with students where they go to purchase school supplies. Ask them if they select the supplies themselves or if a store clerk helps them. Explain to students that in **papelerías** and other smaller stores in Spain much of the merchandise is kept behind the counter.

Viewing

- Have students practice dictation by writing the names of the different articles under Paco's bed as Paco's grandmother finds them. Have students compare lists in pairs.

- Cover the screen and have students listen and write Felipe's telephone number as Paco says the numbers. Then, show the video with picture and have students check their answers.

- Ask students how Paco and his friend Felipe answer the telephone, greet, and say goodbye to each other. You might want to point out that in Spain, **vale** is used to mean "O.K."

Post-viewing

Have students estimate how much the school supplies Paco bought would cost in dollars. Then ask them to convert their estimated prices to euros using the current exchange rate as found on the Internet or in a major newspaper.

Panorama cultural

Pre-viewing

Discuss with students the kinds of supplies they need for school. Ask students to think of ways a list of needed school supplies might vary from country to country. (students may have to buy their own books or school uniforms)

Viewing

- Have students work in pairs. Each pair of students should have various school supplies in front of them. Have students hold up the appropriate school item as it is mentioned in the video. Students should have their backs to the video screen in order not to see the visual clues.

- Point out that Brenda from Mexico, Caroline from Puerto Rico, and Carlos from Mexico are all wearing uniforms. Have students discuss the advantages and disadvantages of wearing a school uniform.

- As students watch the video, have them point out the words used by the interviewees for which they know an alternative term. (**el bulto**, for **la mochila, la libreta** for **el cuaderno, la pluma** for **el bolígrafo**)

- The first **Panorama cultural** activity on Activity Master 3 is based on the first three interviews only.

Post-viewing

Have students compare school supplies they need to begin a new school year with the items the interviewees mention.

Videoclips

- Show the videoclip without sound and ask students if they can guess what this public service message is about. You might wish to tell students that the Spanish word for *literacy* is **alfabetismo**, derived from **alfabeto**.

- Play the videoclip with sound. Have students read the videoclip text on Activity Master 3, p.16 as they listen to the video.

Colorín colorado

- Have students work in pairs to make a list of the inventory they would need to keep on hand if they owned a **papelería** in Spain. They should make the list as extensive as possible. You may wish to replay *¡Mañana es el primer día de clases!* or the **Panorama cultural** when students are finished so they can go back and add items to their lists.

- Have pairs of students take turns playing the roles of a shopkeeper and a customer. The customer should tell the shopkeeper in Spanish what he or she needs to buy in order to start the new school year. The shopkeeper should ask how many of each item the student wants and how much it will cost.

Activity Master 1

De antemano ¡Mañana es el primer día de clases!

Viewing

1. Place a check mark next to the school supplies Paco mentions. He doesn't mention all of them.

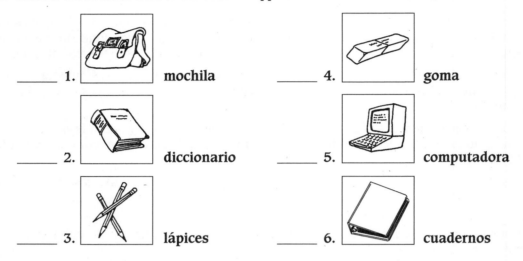

_____ 1. **mochila**	_____ 4. **goma**
_____ 2. **diccionario**	_____ 5. **computadora**
_____ 3. **lápices**	_____ 6. **cuadernos**

2. Who says the following? Write **P** for **Paco** or **A** for **abuela** next to each sentence.

_____ 1. Tengo un nuevo disco compacto de zarzuela.

_____ 2. Mañana es el primer día de clases y necesito muchas cosas.

_____ 3. Primero, organiza tu cuarto.

_____ 4. Compra lo que necesitas. ¡Pero sólo lo que necesitas!

_____ 5. ¿Dónde está el dinero?

Post-viewing

3. For each item, write **necesita** if Paco needed the item for school, **no necesita** if he didn't need it after all, or **quiere** if he just wanted it.

_____ **a.** unos cuadernos

_____ **b.** unos lápices

_____ **c.** una mochila

_____ **d.** un estéreo

_____ **e.** pósters

_____ **f.** papel

Activity Master 2

¡Mañana es el primer día de clases! (a continuación)

> **Supplementary Vocabulary**
> acompañar *to accompany*   el nieto *grandson*
> ¿algo más? *something else?*   el número…*number, shoe size*
> buscar *to look for*

Viewing

1. As you hear them mentioned in the video, circle the letter of each item **abuela** finds in Paco's room. She doesn't mention all of them.

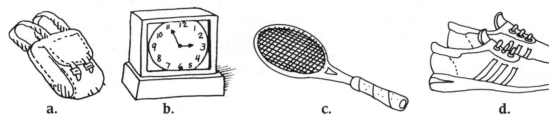

    a.   b.   c.   d.

2. Complete the following phrases with the quantity of each item Paco buys.

_____ cuaderno(s) azul(es)   _____ cuaderno(s) verde(s)

_____ cuaderno(s) rojo(s)   _____ paquete(s) de papel

_____ cuaderno(s) amarillo(s)   _____ gomas

Post-viewing

3. Put the following events in the order in which they take place.

_____ Van a la tienda de discos compactos.

_____ Van a la zapatería.

_____ Paco y Felipe se encuentran en la Plaza de Santa Ana.

_____ Compran papel y gomas.

_____ Regresan a la casa de Paco.

4. Complete the following dialogue by telling the shopkeeper what you need to buy for school.

— Hola, buenas tardes. ¿Qué quieres?

— _____

— Bueno, ¿qué más?

— _____

— ¿Algo más?

— _____

Activity Master 3

Panorama cultural

Supplementary Vocabulary			
el bloc *pad of paper*	la hoja (de papel) *sheet (of paper)*	el pegamento *glue*	los borradores *erasers*
el bulto *backpack*	el/la lapicero/a *pencil case*	el zapato *shoe*	las lapiceras *pens (Arg.)*
la cartera *wallet*	la libreta *notebook*	el uniforme *uniform*	la cartuchera *pencil case (Arg.)*

Viewing

1. Next to each school supply, write the initials (**P, J,** or **F**) of the person who needs to buy them. Three items are needed by more than one student.

    _____ **a.** calculadora _____ **e.** lapiceras _____ **i.** borradores

    _____ **b.** cuadernos _____ **f.** mochila _____ **j.** carpetas

    _____ **c.** cartuchera _____ **g.** libros _____ **k.** gomas

    _____ **d.** lápices _____ **h.** uniforme _____ **l.** reglas

2. The names of some of the school supplies mentioned in the interviews are different from country to country. Match the following words with the places in which they are used.

    _____ **1.** bolígrafo **a.** Puerto Rico

    _____ **2.** pluma **b.** España

    _____ **3.** mochila **c.** Texas

    _____ **4.** bulto **d.** México

Post-viewing

3. List, in Spanish, the items mentioned by the interviewees that you also need for school.

    _____   _____

    _____   _____

    _____   _____

Videoclips

Post-viewing

4. The video says, "**Ya sabes por qué tú has llegado más lejos que él. Léete un libro.**" (*Now you know why you have gone further than he has. Read a book.*) In your opinion, is this effective publicity for persuading people to read? Why or why not? Write your response below.

    _____

    _____

    _____

    _____

CAPÍTULO 2

Location: México

DVD Tutor, Disc 1
Videocassette 1
Start Time: 40:32
Length: 2:30
Pupil's Edition pp. 74–77

The Spanish in the Location Opener is spoken at a normal speed. Students are not expected to understand everything. The activities for this section have been designed to help students understand the major points.

 Teaching Suggestions

 The DVD Tutor contains all video material plus a video-based activity to assess student comprehension after viewing the Location Opener. Short segments are automatically replayed to prompt students if they answer incorrectly.

Pre-viewing

- Ask students to brainstorm and come up with a list of the things they associate with Mexico. List their responses on a transparency or on the board. You might prompt them with some categories, such as foods, music, landscapes, history, industry, etc.

- Ask students to locate **México, D.F.** and **Taxco** on the map on p. xxviii of the *Pupil's Edition*. You might want to point out the two great mountain ranges running through Mexico from the United States to Guatemala: **la Sierra Madre Occidental** and **la Sierra Madre Oriental**. About half of Mexico's population lives in the central highlands, between the two mountain ranges.

Viewing

- Show the video without sound. Have students write a list of the things they see in the video. Then have students compare that list with the one they made before watching the video.

- While showing the video without sound, give students background information about some of the places that are shown. Explain to students that Mexico City was built by the Aztecs in the mid-1300s and was called **Tenochtitlán**. It was a city of more than 100,000 by 1519 when the Spaniards arrived. It is now one of the most populous cities in the world with more than 20 million inhabitants. Point out the pyramids (**la pirámide del sol** and **la pirámide de la luna**) in **Teotihuacán**, located about 30 miles from Mexico City. **Teotihuacán** developed more than 2,000 years ago and eventually reached a population of 100,000. By the time the Aztecs arrived, it was an ancient ruin. Nobody knows what caused the destruction of this city.

- Show the video with sound. Ask students to complete the activities on Activity Master, p. 18. You may need to show the video more than once.

Post-viewing

- Have students work with a partner to compare their answers to Activities 1, 2, and 3 on p. 18. If necessary, play the video again.

- Ask students how their image of Mexico has changed after seeing the video. Ask them if there were any surprises and if some of their expectations were confirmed.

- Ask students to list some aspects of Mexican life pictured in the Location Opener that they would now like to learn more about. You may wish to have students work in small groups and find out as much as they can about the aspect of Mexican life they chose. Have them report what they find to the class.

Activity Master: Location Opener

┌───┐
│   **Supplementary Vocabulary**   │
│ el acero *steel*   pintoresco/a *picturesque* │
│ la artesanía *handicrafts*   la platería *silversmithing*│
│ el caleidoscopio *kaleidoscope*   los recursos naturales *natural resources* │
│ el habitante *inhabitant*   el sabor *taste*   │
│ hecho/a *made*   el son *sound*   │
│ indígeno/a *indigenous; native to a place or region*   │
└───┘

Viewing

1. Place a check mark next to the items that are made in Mexico, according to the video.

   _____ 1. automóviles   _____ 3. acero   _____ 5. castillos

   _____ 2. caleidoscopios   _____ 4. energía eléctrica _____ 6. aviones

Post-viewing

2. Write **C** for **cierto** or **F** for **falso** in the space next to each item.

   _____ 1. La capital de México es la ciudad más grande del mundo.

   _____ 2. La capital de México tiene 10 millones de habitantes.

   _____ 3. La capital de México es famosa por su platería.

   _____ 4. Varias civilizaciones indígenas construyeron grandes ciudades.

   _____ 5. México es un país rico por sus recursos naturales.

3. Choose the sentence which best describes each of the following pictures.

   a. Varias civilizaciones indígenas construyeron grandes ciudades.

   b. La capital de México es la ciudad más grande del mundo.

   c. Las distintas culturas han formado un caleidoscopio de sones, ritmos y colores.

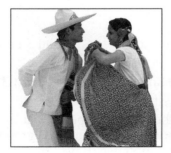  

   1. _____   2. _____   3. _____

Spanish 1 ¡Ven conmigo!

Nuevas clases, nuevos amigos

Functions modeled in video:

The DVD Tutor provides instant access to any part of the video program as well as the ability to repeat short segments as needed. The DVD Tutor also allows access to Spanish-language captions for all video segments as well as to video-based comprehension activities to assess student comprehension.

- talking about classes and sequencing events
- telling time
- telling at what time something happens
- talking about being late or in a hurry
- describing people and things
- talking about things you like and explaining why

Video Segment	Correlation to Print Materials			Videocassette 1		Videocassette 5 (captioned)	
	Pupil's Edition	Video Guide		Start Time	Length	Start Time	Length
		Activity Masters	Scripts				
De antemano	pp. 80–81	p. 22	pp. 91–92	43:03	5:29	0:22:05	5:29
A continuación		p. 23	pp. 92–93	48:34	5:16	0:27:36	5:21
Panorama cultural	p. 87	p. 24	p. 93	53:51	3:01		
Videoclips		p. 24	p. 93	56:53	0:51		

Video Synopses

De antemano ¡Bienvenida al colegio!

Claudia is starting the year at a new school. She meets the school principal, who introduces her to the students in her first class. While waiting for her teacher to arrive, Claudia talks with her new classmates, Fernando and María Inés. María Inés jokingly begins to imitate the teacher in front of the class, not realizing that he is standing in the doorway of the classroom.

¡Bienvenida al colegio! (a continuación)

María Inés receives an extra assignment from her teacher. After school, Fernando and María Inés introduce Claudia to some of their friends, including Luis. Claudia, Luis, and María Inés decide to go to the park to buy popsicles.

Panorama cultural ¿Cómo es un día escolar típico?

- Students from Costa Rica, Argentina, and Venezuela tell what a typical school day is like for them.
- In additional interviews, students from various Spanish-speaking countries tell us about their school day.

Videoclips

I.C.E.: advertisement for lower telephone rates during the holidays

The DVD Tutor contains all video material plus video-based activities to assess student comprehension of **De antemano, A continuación,** and **Panorama cultural.** Short video segments are automatically replayed to prompt students if they answer incorrectly.

De antemano ¡Bienvenida al colegio!

Pre-viewing
- Ask students if they have ever had to move to a new place or go to a new school. If so, how did it differ from the school they are in now? Were the teachers and students different from those in their present school? How did the schedules and daily routines differ?
- Ask students to describe their school schedule: number of classes per day, number of subjects studied, hours and length of classes, and grading system.

Viewing
- Play the video without sound. Ask students to compare the school building, students, and teachers in the video with those at their school. Ask students what similarities and differences they see.
- Mention that many schools in Latin America have classroom doors opening onto an outdoor patio, like the one in the video.
- Play the video with sound. Ask students to listen for the three Mexican slang expressions: **¡Qué padre!, ¡Híjole!,** and **¡No hombre!** Ask them to guess what they mean. (Cool!, Oh brother!, No way!)
- Before directing students to Activity 1 on Activity Master 1, p. 22, you may want to ask several global comprehension questions such as: Who is Claudia? What does the principal show her? What is María Inés doing when the teacher enters?

Post-viewing
Have students work in groups of three and describe their favorite and least favorite classes.

¡Bienvenida al colegio! (a continuación)

Pre-viewing
Ask students what consequences they might expect the professor to impose on María Inés for mimicking him in front of the class.

Viewing
- Show the video and ask students what Luis and Claudia have in common. (they both play basketball)
- Show the last scene of the video and point out to the students that Claudia and Luis are teasing María Inés. Ask students what the joke is.

Post-viewing
- Ask students if they have ever been in trouble for doing something similar to what María Inés did. Ask them if they think the disciplinary action she received was fair.
- After completing Activity 3 on Activity Master 2, p. 23, ask students to rewrite the false statements in order to make them true. This can be done individually on a separate piece of paper or as a class, using the board or a transparency to write the new statements.

Spanish 1 ¡Ven conmigo!

Panorama cultural

Pre-viewing

Have students discuss what their school schedules are like. Ask them what they think about going home at midday for lunch.

Viewing

- Point out that Lucía says **mi materia preferida** instead of **mi materia favorita**. Explain that that is another way to say the same thing.

- Play the interviews with **Gala, Juan,** and **Lucila**. Ask students at what time each of the interviewees begins his or her school day. Have students calculate how many hours a day **Gala** is in school.

- The first **Panorama cultural** activity on Activity Master 3 is based on the first three interviews only.

Post-viewing

Have students watch the interviews and decide whose schedule they would prefer to have and why.

Videoclips

- Show the videoclip without sound and ask students to guess what the commercial is promoting. (reduced rates for long distance calls during the Christmas holidays)

- Play the videoclip with sound and ask students to compare the pace of the visuals in the commercial before and after they hear ¡**deténgase**! Have them try to guess what this word means based on the fact that the pace of the visuals slows down.

Colorín colorado

Have students work in small groups to role-play a situation in which a new student comes into class. Have students introduce themselves, describe their Spanish class, and ask the new student about his or her schedule. You may want to replay *¡Bienvenida al colegio!* first and have students write the words Luis and María Inés use to describe their classes (**horrible, aburrido, mucha tarea, difíciles, es mi favorita, interesante**).

Activity Master 1

De antemano ¡Bienvenida al colegio!

Supplementary Vocabulary		
es de muy buena onda ... *is a nice person*	el horario *schedule*	¡Qué padre! *Cool!*
la geometría *geometry*	el museo *museum*	la química *chemistry*

Viewing

1. Read the following statements before you begin watching the video. Then, as you watch, place a check mark next to the statements that are true.

_____ 1. La clase de ciencias sociales es a las ocho.

_____ 2. La nueva estudiante se llama Claudia Obregón Sánchez.

_____ 3. Claudia es de Cuernavaca.

_____ 4. A Claudia le gustan los museos.

_____ 5. Al amigo de Fernando le gusta jugar al básquetbol.

_____ 6. A María Inés no le gusta mucho la clase de ciencias sociales.

Post-viewing

2. Match the following dialogues with the corresponding pictures.

1. _____   2. _____   3. _____   4. _____

— Mira. Me gusta ir al parque con mi familia y también me gusta visitar los museos. Son buenos.	— Bueno, ya son las ocho menos cinco. ¿Lista? — Sí. — ¿Qué te pasa, Claudia? ¿Estás nerviosa?	— Buenos días, profesor Romanca. — Buenos días, profesor Altamirano. ¿Está aquí la nueva estudiante?	— Sr. Rodríguez, una pregunta. ¿Le gustan las ciencias sociales? — Sí, profesor, me gustan.
a.	b.	c.	d.

3. Match the following video characters with the statements.

1. Claudia   a. No le gusta la clase de ciencias sociales.

2. María Inés   b. Le gustan mucho los museos.

3. Fernando   c. Llega un poco tarde a clase.

4. Profesor Romanca   d. La clase de ciencias sociales es su favorita.

Spanish 1 ¡Ven conmigo!

Activity Master 2

¡Bienvenida al colegio! (a continuación)

Pre-viewing

1. Look at the picture of María Inés, Claudia, Fernando, and Luis. What do you think they are saying?

Supplementary Vocabulary	
la actriz *actress*	las paletas *popsicles*
el básquet *basketball*	responsable *responsable*

_____

_____

_____

_____

_____

Viewing

2. Choose a sentence from the box to complete the following dialogues.

1. — _____
   — Hola. Bienvenida a Cuernavaca.

2. — _____
   — Se llama Luis. Es muy simpático.

3. — ¿Juegas mucho al básquet?
   — _____

4. — Muchas veces, hay 50 estudiantes en una sola clase.
   — _____
   — Allá, es normal.

> a. ¿Quién es ese chico alto con Fernando?
>
> b. Sí. En mi colegio en la capital, jugaba todos los días.
>
> c. ¡Qué difícil!
>
> d. Les presento a una compañera nueva.

Post-viewing

3. Write **C** for **cierto** or **F** for **falso** in the space next to each item.

_____ 1. María Inés tiene una tarea adicional muy fácil.

_____ 2. Después del colegio, los chicos van a casa de Claudia.

_____ 3. El amigo de Fernando se llama Luis.

_____ 4. A Claudia y a Luis les gusta jugar al básquet.

_____ 5. Los colegios en la Ciudad de México son más grandes que los de Cuernavaca, pero las clases son más fáciles.

CAPÍTULO 3

Nombre _____ Clase _____ Fecha _____

Activity Master 3

Panorama cultural

Supplementary Vocabulary

el horario *schedule*

humanístico/a *of the humanities, arts, and history*

me acuesto *I lie down*

preferido/a *favorite*

Viewing

1. Based on the interviews, complete the following sentences with the correct times.

   MARIO En el horario de la mañana voy a las _____ de la mañana y en el horario

   de la tarde a las _____.

   NATALIE Voy a la escuela de _____ de la mañana a _____ de la tarde.

   Después me acuesto como hasta las _____ de la tarde.

2. Draw hands on the clocks below to indicate at what time Gala, Juan, and Lucila say the following events happen.

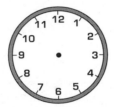      

Gala: salgo a almorzar   Juan: empiezan las clases   Lucila: nos vamos a comer

Videoclips

Supplementary Vocabulary

al *to the*

desde *from*

diciembre *December*

disfruta de sus fiestas *enjoy your holidays*

enero *January*

Feliz Navidad *Merry Christmas*

también *also, too*

las tarifas superreducidas *super-reduced rates*

Viewing

3. Circle the times that appear on the clocks in the videoclip.

   a. 10:00   **b.** 11:00   **c.** 4:00   **d.** 5:00   **e.** 2:00

4. Write the dates and times for the **tarifas superreducidas** in the spaces provided.

   Desde el _____ de diciembre, de las _____

   de la noche, hasta las _____ de la mañana del

   _____ de enero.

Spanish 1 ¡Ven conmigo!

CAPÍTULO 3

¿Qué haces esta tarde?

Functions modeled in video:

 The DVD Tutor provides instant access to any part of the video program as well as the ability to repeat short segments as needed. The DVD Tutor also allows access to Spanish-language captions for all video segments as well as to video-based comprehension activities to assess student comprehension.

- talking about what you like to do
- discussing what you and others do during free time
- telling where people and things are
- talking about where you and others go during free time

Video Segment	Correlation to Print Materials			Videocassette 2		Videocassette 5 (captioned)	
	Pupil's Edition	Video Guide		Start Time	Length	Start Time	Length
		Activity Masters	Scripts				
De antemano	pp. 110–111	p. 28	pp. 93–94	1:15	6:43	0:32:58	6:43
A continuación		p. 29	pp. 94–95	8:00	7:35	0:39:42	7:38
Panorama cultural	p. 122*	p. 30	p. 95	15:53	1:50		
Videoclips		p. 30	p. 95	17:43	0:57		

 Video Synopses

De antemano ¿Dónde está María Inés?

Claudia and Luis plan to go to Taxco with Claudia's sister Rosa. Knowing that María Inés enjoys Taxco, Claudia and Luis decide to invite her to go with them. They look for María Inés at all the places she usually goes on Saturdays. Unfortunately they miss her by just a few minutes at each place.

¿Dónde está María Inés? (a continuación)

After failing to find María Inés, Claudia and Luis return to Claudia's house, where María Inés meets up with them. They go sightseeing in Taxco and visit Claudia's uncle, a local silversmith. He makes a special gift for Claudia to take back for her mother's birthday.

Panorama cultural ¿Te gusta pasear con tus amigos?

- Teenagers from California, Argentina, Mexico, and Spain talk about enjoying the **paseo**.
- In additional interviews, people from various Spanish-speaking countries tell their opinions about the **paseo**.

Videoclips

Banco popular: advertisement by bank promoting respect for people with disabilities.

The DVD Tutor contains all video material plus video-based activities to assess student comprehension of **De antemano, A continuación,** and **Panorama cultural.** Short video segments are automatically replayed to prompt students if they answer incorrectly.

De antemano ¿Dónde está María Inés?

Pre-viewing

Ask students what they usually do on Saturdays. What are the places people might look if they wanted to find them on a Saturday?

Viewing

• Ask students which days of the week Claudia sings in the choir with Luis. (**los martes y los jueves**) On which days does Claudia's father at first think they sing? (**los miércoles y los viernes**)

• Have students make a list of the different places where Claudia, Luis, and María Inés go.

Post-viewing

• Have students make a map showing María Inés' path. Students may number each place where she goes and connect the place with lines. You may wish to play the video again so students can check and make corrections to their map.

• Ask students where they think María Inés will go next, and what they think Claudia and Luis will do.

¿Dónde está María Inés? (a continuación)

Pre-viewing

Ask students to locate Taxco on the map on p. xxviii of the *Pupil's Edition*. Tell students that Taxco is a beautiful city nestled in the mountains of the **Sierra Madre del Sur**, about halfway between Mexico City and the Pacific coastal city of Acapulco. Since colonial times, Taxco has been a center of silver mining and artistry. Mexico is the world's leading exporter of silver.

Viewing

• Ask students why the four characters don't find **tío Ernesto** at home when they first arrive in Taxco. Ask them what they do while waiting for him to arrive.

• Play both the first and second acts and have students focus on Cuernavaca in the first act and Taxco in the second.

Post-viewing

• After students have completed post-viewing Activity 3, have them rewrite the false items to make them true.

• The video presents many opportunities to launch research reports about Taxco and the craft of silverworking. You may want to ask students to pick one aspect of Taxco mentioned in the video (**La Feria de la Plata, la iglesia de la Santa Prisca**) for further research.

Spanish 1 ¡Ven conmigo!

Panorama cultural

Pre-viewing
- Discuss the **paseo** with students, and how it may take different forms in a large city or a small town, just as "hanging out" may differ from place to place in the United States. Describe how towns and cities in the Spanish-speaking world are traditionally built around a central plaza, where people go for walks each evening to "see and be seen."
- Have students make a list of the places where they like to go when they go for walks or "hang out" with friends.

Viewing
- Have students listen to the interviews and make a list of the places each of the interviewees go.
- Ask students how the place Kevin goes on his **paseo** is a reflection of where he lives. Discuss with students how geographical location influences the **paseo**.
- The first **Panorama cultural** activity on Activity Master 3 is based on the first four interviews only.

Post-viewing
Have students compare the list of places that they go with the list of places the interviewees goes. Ask them which places they think are more interesting.

Videoclips

- As students view the video, ask them to notice what part of the dancers and the piano player are the most frequent images seen. (feet of dancers, hands of piano player)
- Have students hypothesize about the message of the commercial, using the images of feet and hands as clues to the meaning of what the announcer is saying. Tell them to listen for the words **manos** and **pies** in the commercial.

Colorín colorado

Have students work in small groups to role-play a situation in which they are searching for a friend. Have them use actual names of places in their town or school. You may want to replay *¿Dónde está María Inés?* and pause at the scene in which the characters talk about what María Inés likes to do and at the scene in which Felipe and Claudia are looking for María Inés and have students begin their role-playing at those points.

Activity Master 1

De antemano ¿Dónde está María Inés?

Supplementary Vocabulary

la alberca *swimming pool*	¿Me acompañas? *Will you accompany me?*
el baile folklórico *folk dance*	la plata *silver*
el cumpleaños *birthday*	el/la platero,-a *silversmith*
no hay remedio *there is no other way*	

Pre-viewing

1. What do you like to do on Saturdays? Look at the following free time activities and rate them by writing 1, 2, or 3.

> **1 = aburrido   2 = interesante   3 = divertido**

a. _____

b. _____

c. _____

d. _____

e. _____

f. _____

Viewing

2. Look at the following list of activities and circle those that are mentioned in the video.

   a. cantar en el coro
   b. ir a la alberca
   c. estudiar en la biblioteca

   d. mirar la televisión
   e. pasear en bicicleta
   f. tocar la guitarra

   g. jugar al básquetbol
   h. caminar con el perro
   i. lavar el carro

Post-viewing

3. Put the following events in the order in which they take place in the video.

   a. _____ Claudia y Luis están en la biblioteca.

   b. _____ María Inés está en la escuela de baile.

   c. _____ Luis está en la casa de Claudia.

   d. _____ Claudia y Luis están en la escuela de baile.

   e. _____ María Inés está en el correo.

   f. _____ Claudia y Luis están en la tienda.

Activity Master 2

¿Dónde está María Inés? (a continuación)

Supplementary Vocabulary		
el desfile *parade*	la iglesia *church*	sacar una foto *to take a photo*
la feria *fair*	la pieza *piece*	el teleférico *cable car*

Viewing

1. Complete the dialogue below with the letter of the correct word from the word box.

   > **a. Taxco   c. correo   e. escuela**
   > **b. casa   d. biblioteca**

   CLAUDIA María Inés no está en la _____ de baile,

   no está en el _____ y no está aquí en

   la _____. ¿Qué hacemos?

   LUIS Bueno, no sé. Vamos a _____ a la una,

   ¿no?

   CLAUDIA No hay remedio. Vamos a _____.

2. Place a check mark next to the events that happen in the video.

   _____ **a.** María Inés va a la casa de Claudia.

   _____ **b.** María Inés llama a su mamá.

   _____ **c.** Claudia, Rosa, María Inés y Luis juegan al fútbol con tío Ernesto.

   _____ **d.** Rosa camina con el perro de tío Ernesto.

   _____ **e.** Claudia, Luis y María Inés van al teleférico.

   _____ **f.** Claudia habla por teléfono con tío Ernesto.

   _____ **g.** Tío Ernesto tiene un regalo para la mamá de Claudia.

   _____ **h.** Tío Ernesto regresa a Cuernavaca a las cinco de la tarde.

Post-viewing

3. Based on what you saw in the video, write **C** for **cierto** or **F** for **falso** in the space beside each item.

   _____ 1. Rosa, Claudia, María Inés y Luis llegan tarde a Taxco.

   _____ 2. Las piezas de plata para la madre de Rosa y Claudia son bonitas.

   _____ 3. Taxco está muy lejos de Cuernavaca.

   _____ 4. A Luis le gusta Taxco.

CAPÍTULO 4

Activity Master 3

Panorama cultural

Supplementary Vocabulary		
el calor *heat*	el lugar *place*	se pasa bien *one has a good time*
hacerse amigos *to make friends*	la manera *way*	pasear *to go for a walk*

Viewing

1. Match each person with the reason he or she likes the **paseo**.

  _____ 1. Patricia   **a.** Podemos ir de la casa de uno o a la casa de otro.

  _____ 2. David   **b.** Es una manera de hacerse más amigos de todos.

  _____ 3. Juan Pablo   **c.** Me gusta ir al parque para ver a los muchachos.

  _____ 4. Jimena   **d.** Se pasa bien aquí con los amigos.

2. Write **C** for **cierto** or **F** for **falso** in the space next to each item.

  _____ **a.** A Patricia le gusta ir a las tiendas.

  _____ **b.** A David le gusta pasear con su familia.

  _____ **c.** Juan Pablo va a María Luisa.

  _____ **d.** Jimena va a muchos lugares.

  _____ **e.** Jeimmy y sus compañeros pasean juntos.

  _____ **f.** Para Leslie el paseo es aburrido.

  _____ **g.** A Claudia le gusta pasear con la familia.

  _____ **h.** Kevin va al parque.

Post-viewing

3. Rewrite the false statements in Activity 1 to make them true.

  _____

  _____

  _____

  _____

  _____

Videoclips

Supplementary Vocabulary	
apoye el teletón *support the telethon*	ningún hombre *no man (or person)*
con las manos *with one's hands*	se pueden mover los pies *the feet can be moved*
menos válido que otro *less important than another*	ya lo está haciendo *is already doing so*

Viewing

4. Place a check mark next to the activities that you see. Not all activities are shown.

  _____ **a.** descansar en el parque   _____ **c.** bailar

  _____ **b.** tocar el piano   _____ **d.** montar en bicicleta

Location: Florida

DVD Tutor, Disc 1
Videocassette 2
Start Time: 18:54
Length: 2:02
Pupil's Edition pp. 136–139

The Spanish in the Location Opener is spoken at a normal speed. Students are not expected to understand everything. The activities for this section have been designed to help students understand the major points.

 Teaching Suggestions

 The DVD Tutor contains all video material plus a video-based activity to assess student comprehension after viewing the Location Opener. Short segments are automatically replayed to prompt students if they answer incorrectly.

Pre-viewing

- Ask if any students have ever been to Florida. Have students name some of the things they would like to see and do in Florida. List their responses on a transparency or on the board.

- Ask students to locate Miami on the map on p. xxvix of the *Pupil's Edition*. Point out that Miami is only 150 miles from Havana, Cuba. Tell students that there is a section of Miami called Little Havana, or **la Pequeña Habana**. Over a million people of Cuban ancestry live in southeastern Florida. You may wish to explain to students that many Cubans have come to Miami as political refugees since Fidel Castro's revolution in 1959. Although Miami is often noted for its Cuban American community, the city is a hub of business and cultural activity with links to all of Latin America.

- Ask students to think of a Spanish word that might be related to the name of Florida (**flor**), and to take a guess at what **florida** means. (full of flowers) Explain that the first Europeans to see Florida were Spaniards. Students may refer to the map of New Spain on p. 3 of the *Pupil's Edition* to see that New Spain included the land that is now Florida. You may wish to tell students about the explorer Ponce de León who landed in Florida in 1513 in search of a mythical fountain of youth.

Viewing

- Play the video and ask students to list what places they see that they would like to visit, and to say why. (beach, aquatic park, shopping in Miami)

- Play the video again and have students complete Activities 1, 2, and 3 on the Activity Master, p. 32. You may need to play the video more than once.

Post-viewing

- Ask students if there were any places or things to do in Florida on the video that they had not expected. If they were to shoot an alternate version of the Location Opener, what scenes would they include? Why?

- Have students work with a partner or in small groups to compare their answers to Activities 1, 2, and 3 on p. 32. If necessary, play the video again.

Activity Master: Location Opener

Supplementary Vocabulary

agradable *pleasant*	los hispanohablantes *Spanish speakers*
el ambiente cosmopolita *cosmopolitan or international atmosphere*	el hogar *home*
	los locales *places of business*
el clima *climate*	uno de los lugares más alegres *one of the liveliest places*
las comunidades étnicas *ethnic communities*	se habla español *Spanish is spoken*
los familiares *relatives*	las tiendas *stores*

Viewing

1. The video gives four reasons why Florida has more visitors than almost any other state. Place a check mark next to each of the reasons mentioned.

   La Florida es uno de los estados más visitados…

   _____ **a.** por su agradable clima   _____ **d.** por sus parques

   _____ **b.** por sus hermosas playas   _____ **e.** por las pirámides de los mayas

   _____ **c.** por sus montañas   _____ **f.** por su ambiente cosmopolita

Post-viewing

2. In the blank to the left of each statement, write **C** for **cierto** or **F** for **falso**. If a statement is false, rewrite it in the space below so that it becomes true.

   _____ **a.** Muchos turistas visitan la Florida.

   _____ **b.** La mayoría de los hispanohablantes son mexicanos.

   _____ **c.** En la Pequeña Habana hay muchas playas.

   _____ **d.** En las tiendas y restaurantes de la Pequeña Habana se habla español.

   _____ **e.** Miami tiene grandes comunidades centroamericanas y sudamericanas.

3. Choose the most appropriate word from the word bank to complete the description of the picture.

cosmopolita	estados	revista
clima	carro	playas

   La Florida es uno de los _____ más

   visitados, por su agradable _____,

   sus hermosas _____ y su

   ambiente _____.

El ritmo de la vida

CAPÍTULO 5

Functions modeled in video:

The DVD Tutor provides instant access to any part of the video program as well as the ability to repeat short segments as needed. The DVD Tutor also allows access to Spanish-language captions for all video segments as well as to video-based comprehension activities to assess student comprehension.

- discussing how often you do things
- talking about what you and your friends like to do together
- talking about what you do during a typical week
- giving today's date
- talking about the weather

Video Segment	Correlation to Print Materials			Videocassette 2		Videocassette 5 (captioned)	
	Pupil's Edition	Video Guide		Start Time	Length	Start Time	Length
		Activity Masters	Scripts				
De antemano	pp. 142–143	p. 36	p. 96	20:58	4:06	0:47:21	4:06
A continuación		p. 37	p. 96	25:04	4:33	0:51:29	4:36
Panorama cultural	p. 153*	p. 38	p. 97	29:37	3:00		
Videoclips		p. 38	p. 97	32:27	0:51		

 ## Video Synopses

De antemano ¿Cómo es el ritmo de tu vida?

In this episode, students in Miami prepare a news broadcast program for their high school. José Luis gives the national weather forecast, and Raquel interviews students about what they do during their free time. After Raquel's last interview, there is a problem with the camera in the studio and the broadcast is interrupted.

¿Cómo es el ritmo de tu vida? (a continuación)

The students resolve the camera problem and finish their news broadcast. The next day they show Armando, the new student from Panama, the gardens of Vizcaya.

Panorama cultural ¿Cómo es una semana típica?

- Teenagers from Ecuador, Venezuela, and Argentina tell us what they usually do during the week and on weekends.
- In additional interviews, people from various Spanish-speaking countries tell us what a typical week is like for them.

Videoclips

Pronóstico del tiempo: weather report from Costa Rica

Teaching Suggestions

The DVD Tutor contains all video material plus video-based activities to assess student comprehension of **De antemano, A continuación,** and **Panorama cultural.** Short video segments are automatically replayed to prompt students if they answer incorrectly.

De antemano ¿Cómo es el ritmo de tu vida?

Pre-viewing

Ask students to imagine creating a monthly video program for teenagers. Have students work in groups and decide what features and special interest reports they would include (weather, interviews, news, etc.), where would they shoot the video (in a studio, on location), and what role each group member would like to play (host, reporter, writer, camera person).

Viewing

- Show the video without sound. Ask students what the weather is like in Miami, New York, Chicago, California, and Texas, using the icons that José Luis points to in his forecast as clues. Then, play the video with sound and have students listen for the Spanish weather expressions that José Luis uses.

- Ask students to make a list of the free time activities mentioned by the people Raquel interviews.

Post-viewing

- Ask students which of the free time activities mentioned in Raquel's interviews they consider the most interesting, and why.

- Have students write a postcard to Raquel (as requested in the video). In the postcard, they should introduce themselves, answer Raquel's question "**¿Les gusta el programa?**", and tell her about their favorite pastimes.

¿Cómo es el ritmo de tu vida? (a continuación)

Pre-viewing

Ask students to name some clubs or community service projects at their school and tell about what those clubs do.

Viewing

- Ask students why they think Patricia and José Luis look nervous. Ask them why they keep repeating the phrase **hace mucho calor.** (to buy time while they look for their notes)

- Have students make a chart like the one below. Then, have them listen to the video and fill in the names of the two clubs mentioned (**ecología, ciencias**), where they are going to meet (**el colegio, el planetario**) and when they are going to meet (**el sábado a las diez, el sábado a las tres**).

Club		
¿Dónde?		
¿Cuándo?		

- Tell students that the Vizcaya is an Italian Renaissance-style mansion surrounded by nature trails and gardens. It was completed in 1916.

Post-viewing

Teach your students the Spanish names for some of the clubs at their school and have them tell you when they meet. Then have them work in small groups to role-play making announcements about the meetings. You may want to replay *¿Cómo es el ritmo de tu vida? (a continuación)*.

Panorama cultural

Pre-viewing

Have students conduct a class survey on what they do during a typical week and what they do on weekends. Tally the responses and have students look for similarities and differences. Ask students if they think young people from Spanish-speaking countries do the same types of things.

Viewing

- Have students make a list of the activities that Matías, María Luisa, and Maikel do during the week and on weekends. Ask students which activity they have in common. (going to school)

- Ask students to listen for different ways of saying *school* (**colegio, liceo, escuela**). Then have students note which words are used in which countries (**colegio** in Argentina and Ecuador; **liceo** in Venezuela; **escuela** in El Salvador).

- The first **Panorama cultural** activity on Activity Master 3 is based on the first three interviews only.

Post-viewing

Have students compare the list of their activities and the list of activities of the people interviewed. Ask them to point out the similarities and differences.

Videoclips

- Show the videoclip without sound and have students guess what it is. (a weather report)

- Have students locate Costa Rica on the map on p. xxvii of the *Pupil's Edition*. If you have an atlas map of Costa Rica, ask students to locate the five regions shown in the videoclip: **el Valle Central, Liberia, Puntarenas, la zona norte,** and **Limón.** You might want to point out that **Liberia** is in the province of **Guanacaste, Puntarenas** is on the Pacific coast (**el sector pacífico**), and **Limón** is on the Caribbean coast (**la vertiente del Caribe**).

- Show the videoclip and ask students if the temperatures for each region are given before or after the weather conditions. Replay the video if students don't agree on the answer. (temperatures are given at end of each report)

- Play the video a few times and ask students to write down any familiar words or cognates they hear. They may catch **el instituto meteorológico, el tiempo, nublado, la temperatura.**

- Have students compare the temperatures given in the weather report to current local temperatures, changing degrees centigrade to degrees Fahrenheit if necessary. Ask if it's possible to determine the season in Costa Rica solely from the temperature report. (No, since Costa Rica is close to the equator, the temperature is fairly constant year-round.)

Colorín colorado

- Have students work in small groups and create a video program like **Noticias Colegio Seminole** for their school. Have them give a weather report, make announcements about club meetings, and interview several people in their school about their favorite free-time activities. If possible, make a video of the presentations and share them with other Spanish classes.

- Replay the segment of Raquel's special TV report in *¿Cómo es el ritmo de tu vida?* without sound. Have students play the parts of Raquel and the people she interviews by providing narration while the video plays. Encourage students to improvise.

Activity Master 1

De antemano ¿Cómo es el ritmo de tu vida?

Pre-viewing

1. The following Spanish words are all cognates. Write their English equivalents in the spaces provided.

Supplementary Vocabulary	
los grados *degrees*	el reportaje *report*
la pulgada *inch*	la temperatura *temperature*

_____ 1. edición

_____ 2. programa

_____ 3. temperatura

_____ 4. reportaje

_____ 5. actividades

_____ 6. cámara

Viewing

2. Decide which pictures best illustrate the weather in the following locations according to José Luis' forecast.

   a. viento   b. lluvia   c. sol   d. nieve   e. frío

_____ 1. Miami   _____ 3. Chicago   _____ 5. Texas

_____ 2. Nueva York   _____ 4. California

3. Circle the activities that are mentioned by each of the following characters. There may be more than one activity for each character.

   1. Ramón: **a.** hacer la tarea   **b.** trabajar en un   **c.** nadar en una piscina
                                                          restaurante

   2. Anita: **a.** descansar   **b.** leer el periódico   **c.** hablar con mi hermana

   3. Josué: **a.** comer helado   **b.** correr   **c.** bucear

   4. Profesor Williams: **a.** preparar la cena   **b.** escribir cartas   **c.** estudiar matemáticas

4. Complete the following information about the new student Armando.

   Armando es de 1. _____ .

   Su apellido es 2. _____ .

   En su tiempo libre, a Armando le gusta 3. _____ y 4. _____ .

Activity Master 2

¿Cómo es el ritmo de tu vida? (a continuación)

Supplementary Vocabulary

el aire acondicionado *air conditioning*   el jardín *garden*   el planetario *planetarium*

el estudio *studio*   el letrero *sign*   el voluntario *volunteer*

la flor *flower*   el planeta *planet*

Viewing

1. Circle the names of the two school clubs that are mentioned in the video.

   Club de historia   Club de ciencias

   Club de ecología   Club de literatura

2. Choose the correct completion for each of the sentences below.

   _____ 1. Hace calor...

   _____ 2. Nuestro Club de ecología necesita...

   _____ 3. Vamos a ver un programa especial sobre...

   _____ 4. ¿Qué vamos a...

   _____ 5. ¿Por qué no vamos al...

   a. el planeta Júpiter.

   b. hacer mañana?

   c. en Miami.

   d. voluntarios este sábado.

   e. Museo Vizcaya?

Post-viewing

3. Summarize what happens in *¿Cómo es el ritmo de tu vida? (a continuación)* by numbering the following sentences in the correct order.

   _____ **a.** Patricia y José Luis comentan que hace mucho calor.

   _____ **b.** Raquel, Armando, Patricia y José Luis van al Museo Vizcaya.

   _____ **c.** "Noticias Colegio Seminole" tiene algunos problemas técnicos.

   _____ **d.** José Luis informa que el programa sobre el planeta Júpiter es el sábado, a las tres.

   _____ **e.** Todos deciden ir al planetario.

   _____ **f.** Patricia dice que el Club de ecología va a limpiar una sección de la Bahía Bizcayne.

4. Choose one of the clubs at your school and write about an upcoming event by filling in the following announcement. The club may be real or imaginary.

   El Club de _____

   tiene una reunión este _____

   a las _____.

Activity Master 3

Panorama cultural

	Supplementary Vocabulary
andar en velero *to go sailing*	corriente *common*
comer fuera *to go out to dinner*	un montón de cosas *a whole bunch of things*

Viewing

1. Circle the activities that Matías, María Luisa, and Maikel say they do.

   a. comer   **d.** dormir   **g.** jugar al fútbol

   b. nadar   **e.** ir al liceo   **h.** hacer tarea

   c. ver tele   **f.** leer el periódico   **i.** descansar

2. Match the person with the activities he or she does during a typical week by checking the appropriate boxes.

	tocar la guitarra	mirar televisión	trabajar	hacer tarea	ir al Ávila
Lucía					
Marcelo					
Güido					
Jesús					
Juan Fernando					

3. List the names of all of the interviewees who mention that they do homework as part of their typical week.

   _____   _____

   _____   _____

Videoclips

Supplementary Vocabulary	
aisladas lluvias *scattered showers*	nubosidad parcial *partial cloudiness*
aislados aguaceros *scattered showers*	el prognóstico del tiempo *weather forecast*

Viewing

4. Write **sí** next to each statement if it's likely or **no** if it's unlikely, based on the videoclip.

   _____ 1. En el Valle Central hace sol.   _____ 4. En la zona norte llueve.

   _____ 2. En Guanacaste está nublado.   _____ 5. En la vertiente del Caribe hace calor.

   _____ 3. En el sector pacífico hace mucho frío.

Entre familia

Functions modeled in video:

- describing a family
- describing people
- discussing things a family does together
- discussing problems and giving advice

 The DVD Tutor provides instant access to any part of the video program as well as the ability to repeat short segments as needed. The DVD Tutor also allows access to Spanish-language captions for all video segments as well as to video-based comprehension activities to assess student comprehension.

Video Segment	Correlatión to Print Materials			Videocassette 2		Videocassette 5 (captioned)	
	Pupil's Edition	Video Guide		Start Time	Length	Start Time	Length
		Activity Masters	Scripts				
De antemano	pp. 170–171	p. 42	pp. 97–98	33:42	4:09	0:56:06	4:09
A continuación		p. 43	pp. 98–99	37:52	6:22	1:00:17	6:22
Panorama cultural	p. 183*	p. 44	p. 99	44:37	2:56		
Videoclips		p. 44	p. 99	47:33	0:34		

Video Synopses

De antemano ¿Cómo es tu familia?

Armando goes over to Raquel's house and she shows him photos of her family. She describes what her family is like and what they like to do together. While she is showing Armando the photos, they are interrupted by a loud crash.

¿Cómo es tu familia? (a continuación)

Raquel discovers that her dog, Pepe, has come into the house and knocked something over in the other room. She scolds him and sends him outside. Later, she can't find him and is afraid that he has disappeared. After Raquel and her friends scour the neighborhood, they finally find Pepe hiding under a table in Raquel's living room.

Panorama cultural ¿Cuántas personas hay en tu familia?

- Teenagers from Ecuador, Spain, and Texas tell us how many people there are in their family and what they do to help around the house.

- In additional interviews, people from various Spanish-speaking countries tell us about their families and what they do to help around the house.

Videoclips

Estar en familia: public service message supporting spending time with family

The DVD Tutor contains all video material plus video-based activities to assess student comprehension of **De antemano, A continuación,** and **Panorama cultural.** Short video segments are automatically replayed to prompt students if they answer incorrectly.

De antemano ¿Cómo es tu familia?

Pre-viewing
- Have students interview each other about their families, real or imaginary, using the following questions: **¿Cómo es tu familia? ¿Es grande o pequeña? ¿Qué haces con tu familia? ¿Tienen animales domésticos en casa?**
- Ask students to describe what their families might typically eat at a picnic or barbecue.
- Point out to students that Hispanics mostly of Cuban origin make up a large part of the population of Miami. Ask students what things they think they would find in a bilingual community like Miami. (bilingual store signs, newspapers, TV and radio in Spanish, ethnic foods)

Viewing
- Ask students how many brothers and sisters Raquel has. (three brothers and one sister) Then ask how many family members are living at her home. (eight)
- Have students describe the kind of food that Raquel and her family have when they go on a picnic.

Post-viewing
- Point out to students that in Hispanic families it is not unusual to have the extended family living together in one house. Ask students how they would feel about having their extended family living in their home.
- Have students research Cuban cuisine and find recipes for **arroz con frijoles negros**, **maduros**, **tostones**, **pollo asado,** or other typical Cuban dishes. You might even have volunteers prepare a dish for the class.

¿Cómo es tu familia? (a continuación)

Pre-viewing
- Ask students what they think the noise was at the end of the first episode.
- Ask students if they have ever had a family pet get lost. If so, did they eventually find it, and how?

Viewing
Point out that the video characters go to **Calle Ocho** to look for Pepe. **Calle Ocho** is Little Havana's best-known street. Point out the bilingual signs and the fact that people in the video say "Bye!" in addition to **adiós.**

Post-viewing
- Have students write a list of five events from the video in scrambled order. Then have students exchange lists with a partner and try to put them in the correct order.
- Have students role-play a scene in which they describe their lost pet. You may wish to replay the scene in which Raquel describes Pepe to the couple with the baby stroller.

CAPÍTULO 6

Panorama cultural

Pre-viewing

Have students, as a class, create a list of household chores. Then, ask students which chores they think people their age should do. Ask students to vote on the best and worst chore to do.

Viewing

- Ask students what the first three interviewees have in common. (**cinco personas en la familia**)

- Have students pick out which person being interviewed has the most family members and which one has the least. (Éric has the most, and Diego and Paola have the least)

- Ask students who they think helps out around the house the most, and who helps the least.

- The first **Panorama cultural** activity on Activity Master 3 is based on the first three interviews only.

Post-viewing

- Have students work in pairs and ask each other **¿Cuántas personas hay en tu familia?** They should follow Brenda's model, saying what they do to help around the house, and also describing each family member.

- Ask students if they think teenagers in Spanish-speaking families do the same kinds of chores that they do, based on the **Panorama cultural**. Hold a class discussion on this topic.

Videoclips

- Tell students that the videoclip for this chapter is from the west-central Colombian department of Antioquia, whose capital is Medellín. The sponsor of the public service message for this chapter is called IDEA, an acronym for **Instituto para el Desarrollo de Antioquia.**

- Before showing the videoclip, ask students if they can remember any public service messages on television. They may know of ones that stress the importance of an education, avoidance of substance abuse, and the value of being part of a family, among others. Ask students to predict what a brief public service message about family might say.

- Play the videoclip several times so that students can successfully complete Activity 4 on Activity Master 3, p. 44.

- Have students work in small groups and design a public service message in Spanish about the importance of the family. Students can design posters or, if the necessary equipment is available, they can videotape the message.

Colorín colorado

Have students bring in photographs of their family and describe them to the class. Students may prefer to cut out pictures from magazines and describe an imaginary family. You may wish to show *¿Cómo es tu familia?* once more and have students pay attention to the way in which Raquel describes her family.

Activity Master 1

De antemano ¿Cómo es tu familia?

Pre-viewing

1. On a separate sheet of paper, draw a family tree that includes six members of your real or imaginary family. Below each family member's name, write his or her age, relationship to you, and one activity that he or she likes to do.

Supplementary Vocabulary	
el arroz *rice*	los frijoles negros *black beans*
la barbacoa *barbecue*	los maduros *fried plantains*
el/la cocinero,-a *cook*	el pollo asado *baked chicken*
divorciado/a *divorced*	los tostones *fried green plantains*

Viewing

2. Circle the word or phrase that best completes each statement below.

1. La familia de Raquel es _____.
   a. bastante grande   **b.** pequeña   **c.** muy grande

2. _____ vive con la familia de Raquel.
   a. Un abuelo   **b.** Una abuela   **c.** Un tío

3. Los padres de Raquel son de _____.
   a. España   **b.** Puerto Rico   **c.** Cuba

4. A Raquel le gusta la barbacoa de su _____.
   a. papá   **b.** mamá   **c.** abuelo

5. La tía de Raquel _____.
   a. juega al fútbol   **b.** vive con ellos   **c.** toca la flauta

3. Match the following people with activities they like to do. Write all the letters of the activities that correspond to the people in the spaces provided.

1. Raquel _____
2. sus padres _____
3. sus hermanos _____

a. cocinar la barbacoa
b. jugar al fútbol americano
c. comer en el parque
d. trabajar en el jardín
e. tocar la guitarra
f. tocar la flauta

Post-viewing

4. Look at the following picture of Raquel's family and draw her family tree on a separate sheet of paper. Be sure to include the relationship of each member to Raquel, a brief description of each person, and any activities they like to do.

CAPITULO 6

Activity Master 2

¿Cómo es tu familia? (a continuación)

Supplementary Vocabulary

el collar *collar*   nos encontramos *we'll meet each other*
la medalla de identificación *identification tag*   el perro cobrador dorado *golden retriever*

Pre-viewing

1. Interview a partner to find out the following information about him or her.

   Nombre: _____

   Dirección: _____

   _____

   Número de teléfono: _____

Viewing

2. Put the following lines of dialogue from the video in the correct order.

   _____ **a.** Hola, Patricia. Habla Raquel. ¿Está Pepe en frente de tu casa?

   _____ **b.** ¡Qué perro tan perezoso eres, Pepe!

   _____ **c.** Esta puerta siempre está cerrada.

   _____ **d.** Lo siento, Raquel, pero no lo vimos.

   _____ **e.** ¿Qué tal si damos un paseo con Pepe?

Post-viewing

3. Fill in the blanks with words from the word bank to give an accurate description of Pepe.

   1. Pepe es muy _____.

   2. Tiene casi _____ años.

   3. Le gusta _____.

   4. Es bastante _____.

   5. Lleva un collar _____.

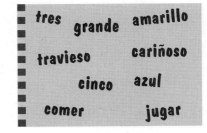

tres grande amarillo
travieso cariñoso
cinco azul
comer jugar

4. Imagine that you've lost the dog in the photo below. Write a description of it. Be sure to include name, address, age, personality, and a physical description.

_____
_____
_____
_____
_____
_____
_____

CAPÍTULO 6

Activity Master 3

Panorama cultural

Supplementary Vocabulary

| barrer *to sweep* | cocinar *to cook* | los quehaceres *chores* |
| rebelde *rebellious* | trapear *to mop* | hacer los trastes *to do the dishes* |

Viewing

1. Match Brenda and her family with their descriptions.

_____ 1. la mamá   **a.** muy bueno

_____ 2. la hermana   **b.** muy protectiva

_____ 3. el hermano   **c.** muy rebelde

_____ 4. el papá   **d.** la más grande de los niños

_____ 5. Brenda   **e.** niño chiquito

2. Write the number of people in each of the following students' families.

_____ **a.** Arantxa   _____ **e.** Diego

_____ **b.** Pablo   _____ **f.** Angie

_____ **c.** Brenda   _____ **g.** Paola

_____ **d.** Éric

3. Check the appropriate boxes to indicate the household chores each of the following people does.

Arantxa				
Éric				
Angie				
Paola				

Videoclips

Supplementary Vocabulary

cierto que *it's true that*   es rico *it's wonderful*

Viewing

4. Fill in the missing words as you listen to the videoclip.

¿Cierto que es muy _____ estar en _____? Porque

en Antioquia _____ rico _____. ¡Cierto!

CAPÍTULO 6

Location Opener for Chapters 7-8

Location: Ecuador

DVD Tutor, Disc 2
Videocassette 3
Start Time: 0:57
Length: 2:27
Pupil's Edition pp. 198–201

The Spanish in the Location Opener is spoken at a normal speed. Students are not expected to understand everything. The activities for this section have been designed to help students understand the major points.

 Teaching Suggestions

> **DVD2** The DVD Tutor contains all video material plus a video-based activity to assess student comprehension after viewing the Location Opener. Short segments are automatically replayed to prompt students if they answer incorrectly.

Pre-viewing

- Ask students what they think Ecuador's name means. Ask students what the equator is. (an imaginary line circling the globe exactly halfway between the north and south poles) Have students locate Ecuador on the world map on pp. xxiv–xxv of the *Pupil's Edition*. Point out that the equator crosses the country. Explain that the sun's rays are most direct near the equator. Ask students how this affects Ecuador's climate. (it's fairly constant year-round)

- Have students look at the map of Ecuador on p. 198 of the *Pupil's Edition*. Explain to them that Ecuador has three distinct land regions: the flat plain of the Coastal Lowlands (**la Costa**), the Andes Highlands (**la Cordillera de los Andes** or **Sierra**), and the thickly forested Eastern Lowlands (**el Oriente**). You may wish to ask students to name the distinct land regions in their state or in the United States. The Galapagos Islands are also part of Ecuador—students may locate these islands on the map on p. xxvi of the *Pupil's Edition*.

- Ask students to locate Quito and Otavalo on the map on p. 198 of the *Pupil's Edition*. Tell students that Quito, the capital of Ecuador, lies on a plateau almost two miles (about three kilometers) above sea level. Ask students what they know about the effects of higher altitudes. (air is thinner, food takes longer to cook) Point out that Quito's high altitude makes its climate much cooler than what would be expected so close to the equator.

Viewing

- Have students write the headings Geography, People, and Architecture on a sheet of paper. Play the video without sound. Under each heading, students should list the contrasts that they observe in the video. (modern buildings vs. traditional buildings, mountains vs. coasts, etc.)

- Show the video again without sound. Tell students that **el volcán Pichincha**, a twin-peaked volcano, rises 4,784 m (15,696 ft.). The lower peak Guagua Pichincha began erupting again in late 1999 for the first time since the mid-seventeenth century. Tell them that Cuenca is also famous for making Panama hats. Point out the ruins of **Ingapirca**. Tell students that **Ingapirca** was constructed by the Incas, whose empire was one of the largest and richest in the Americas. It stretched more than 4,020 km (almost 2500 miles) along the western coast of South America (nearly as long as the United States is wide).

- Show the video with sound and ask students to complete the activities on Activity Master, p. 46. You may need to show the video more than once.

Post-viewing

Ask students to discuss how **"un país de contrastes"** makes Ecuador **"una sociedad dinámica y fascinante"** as stated in the video. Ask them which areas they would be interested in visiting in Ecuador, and why.

Activity Master: Location Opener

Supplementary Vocabulary

la costa *coast*

hace más de quinientos años *more than five hundred years ago*

la historia antigua *ancient history*

la historia contemporánea *recent history*

la joya de los Andes *jewel of the Andes*

las montañas *mountains*

las orillas del río *banks of the river*

la selva *jungle*

sin duda alguna *without any doubt*

las tradiciones *traditions*

el volcán *volcano*

Viewing

1. Place a check mark next to each item as it is mentioned in the video. Some items are not mentioned.

   _____ **a.** las montañas

   _____ **b.** Quito

   _____ **c.** el volcán Pichincha

   _____ **d.** la llama

   _____ **e.** el río Tomebamba

   _____ **f.** Cuenca

   _____ **g.** la Catedral Nueva

   _____ **h.** el castillo

   _____ **i.** las ruinas de Ingapirca

   _____ **j.** Otavalo

2. In the video you learn that Ecuador is "**un país de contrastes**." Match the items on the left with the contrasting item on the right.

   _____ **1.** construcciones modernas

   _____ **2.** historia antigua

   _____ **3.** montañas

   _____ **4.** indígena

   a. europeo

   b. selva y costa

   c. historia contemporánea

   d. arquitectura colonial

Post-viewing

3. Based on what you've learned from the video, write a caption for this picture.

_____

_____

¿Qué te gustaría hacer?

Functions modeled in video:

The DVD Tutor provides instant access to any part of the video program as well as the ability to repeat short segments as needed. The DVD Tutor also allows access to Spanish-language captions for all video segments as well as to video-based comprehension activities to assess student comprehension.

- talking on the telephone
- extending and accepting invitations
- making plans
- talking about getting ready
- turning down an invitation and explaining why

Video Segment	Correlation to Print Materials			Videocassette 3		Videocassette 5 (captioned)	
	Pupil's Edition	Video Guide		Start Time	Length	Start Time	Length
		Activity Masters	Scripts				
De antemano	pp. 204–205	p. 50	p. 100	3:25	5:27	1:06:40	5:26
A continuación		p. 51	pp. 100–101	8:53	5:33	1:12:07	5:39
Panorama cultural	p. 216*	p. 52	p. 101	14:27	2:43		
Videoclips		p. 52	p. 101	17:11	0:45		

Video Synopses

De antemano ¿Qué hacemos?

Tomás tells his friend Carlos that he's in a bad mood because he thinks that he's not invited to María's party. While they are at Carlos's house, María calls Carlos to invite him to the party. Carlos declines the invitation because he already has plans. María then calls Tomás's house and leaves a message inviting him also, but the message gets buried under a stack of books.

¿Qué hacemos? (a continuación)

María runs into Tomás and tells him about the party, so he and Carlos change their plans and decide to go to the party after all. When Tomás and Carlos finally arrive at María's house, she realizes that they weren't told that the party had been postponed until next week. They all end up going out and spending the afternoon together.

Panorama cultural ¿Qué haces para conocer a una persona?

- Students from Ecuador, Costa Rica, and Spain tell us how they would ask someone out and who would pay for the date.

- In additional interviews, people from various Spanish-speaking regions tell us about dating customs.

Videoclips

EDA: advertisement for a telephone company

De antemano ¿Qué hacemos?

Pre-viewing
- Ask students if they were ever not invited to a party that they really wanted to go to. How did they feel and what did they do?
- Tell students that part of the video episode is a phone conversation. Have students mention a few things people commonly say on the phone. (*Is . . . there? May I leave a message?*) Ask them to watch for when the video characters might say these things to each other.

Viewing
- Each time a video character extends an invitation, pause the video and ask students who is extending the invitation, for what reason, and whether or not the person being invited accepts.
- Point out to students that in Ecuador people answer the phone by saying **Aló**. Ask students who are native speakers in your class how they answer the phone in Spanish. Possible responses are **Bueno** and **Diga**.

Post-viewing
- Have students practice leaving phone messages by role-playing a phone conversation in which one student leaves a message with the parent of another student.
- If you have tape recorders available, you may want to let students record answering machine messages in Spanish. First have students record an out-going message explaining why they can't answer the telephone. Then pass the tapes around and have each student leave a message.

¿Qué hacemos? (a continuación)

Pre-viewing
- Have students summarize the first part of the video. Then, ask them what they think will happen in *¿Qué hacemos? (a continuación)*.
- Ask students what time of day they usually have parties and what they usually wear.

Viewing
- Point out to students that it is not unusual for people in Spanish-speaking countries to dress more formally when they get together with friends for a party. Ask students if they would dress the way Tomás and Carlos do when going to a party.
- Ask students to listen for the description of Hiroshi. Ask them where he is from and why he is coming to Quito. (He's an exchange student from San Francisco.)

Post-viewing

Ask students if they think that Tomás should have agreed to go to María's party, knowing that Carlos had declined the invitation and invited him to a concert. Discuss what they would do in the same situation.

Panorama cultural

Pre-viewing

Ask students how teenagers in their community usually ask someone out on a date. Is it acceptable for girls to ask boys? Who usually pays for the date? Do they prefer to go out in groups of friends or as a couple?

Viewing

- Ask students which of the teenagers interviewed have ways of meeting people that are similar to their own.

- Point out to students that when someone says **te invito** it is understood that the person extending the invitation will pay.

- Discuss Manolo's approach to meeting girls. Ask students if they have done anything similar to meet a boy or girl.

- Ask students how many **colones** it usually costs to go on a date in Costa Rica. (mil colones) Use recent currency rates to have students convert **colones** to dollars. Then, ask them how much it would cost in the United States to go out on a typical date.

- The first **Panorama cultural** activity on Activity Master 3 is based on the first three interviews only.

Post-viewing

- After students view the first three interviews, ask them which interviewees prefer to be introduced to a boy or a girl by friends (Jessica and María Isabel), and which one prefers to introduce himself or herself. (Rodrigo)

- Ask students what they think the major differences are between dating in the United States and dating in Spanish-speaking countries.

Videoclips

- Tell students that this videoclip is from Antioquia, Colombia. The people from this department are called **antioqueños**. **EDA**, which produced the commercial, stands for **Empresas Departamentales de Antioquia**, the name of the local phone company.

- Play the videoclip a few times and ask students what they think the young women are talking about before they place the phone call. All theories might be considered equally valid. (They are wondering how Miguel is doing in Bogotá and whether they ought to call him.)

- Ask students to note during which time of the year the commercial takes place. (Christmas) Prompt them to look for visual cues, such as the decorative Christmas lights in the street.

- Have students complete Activities 4 and 5 on Activity Master 3, p. 52. Then ask what the slogan would say if it were advertising in their state. (for Texas it would be **Comunica a los tejanos con el mundo**)

Colorín colorado

Have students role-play a situation in which one student invites another student to a party. Students may either decline or accept the invitation. You may want to replay *¿Qué hacemos?* first and have students write the expressions the characters use to extend or turn down an invitation.

Activity Master 1

De antemano ¿Qué hacemos?

Supplementary Vocabulary
de mal humor *in a bad mood*   el/la estudiante de intercambio *exchange student*

Pre-viewing

1. Complete the following phone conversation by writing the appropriate letter in each space.

TÚ: _____

ALEJO: Hola, hombre, habla Alejo.

TÚ: _____

ALEJO: ¿Quieres ir al cine con Laura y conmigo?

TÚ: _____

> a. ¡Cómo no! Vamos.
>
> b. ¿Aló?
>
> c. Hola, ¿qué pasa?

Viewing

2. Match each person with the phrase he or she says.

   a.   b.   c.   d.

_____ 1. En realidad, prefiero salir. Pero, ¿qué hacemos?

_____ 2. Lo siento, María, pero no puedo. Ya tengo planes.

_____ 3. ¿Puedo dejar un recado, por favor?

_____ 4. Tengo que ponerme los lentes.

Post-viewing

3. Write **C** for **cierto** or **F** for **falso** in the space next to each item.

_____ 1. María va a hacer una fiesta el domingo.

_____ 2. María no quiere invitar a Tomás a la fiesta.

_____ 3. La fiesta es para un estudiante norteamericano.

_____ 4. Tomás y Carlos tienen planes de ir a un concierto.

_____ 5. María habla con el padre de Tomás.

4. Which of the following sentences best summarizes what happened in the video episode?

   a. María hace una fiesta el sábado y Tomás quiere ir.

   b. Un estudiante de intercambio viene a vivir con Carlos y su familia.

   c. Tomás hace una fiesta para un estudiante de intercambio.

Spanish 1 ¡Ven conmigo!

CAPÍTULO 7

Activity Master 2

¿Qué hacemos? (a continuación)

Supplementary Vocabulary	
la fiesta de bienvenida *welcoming party*	¡Qué chévere! *How cool!*
la guagua *baby (Ecuador, Chile)*	la sandía *watermelon*

Pre-viewing

1. Look at the pictures in Activity 2 below. What do you think will happen in *¿Qué hacemos? (a continuación)*? Circle the answer.

   a. Tomás no recibe el recado de María y va al concierto con Carlos.

   b. Tomás acepta la invitación de María y va a la fiesta pero Carlos va al concierto.

   c. Tomás recibe el recado de María y luego Carlos y Tomás van a la fiesta.

   d. Tomás recibe el recado de María pero decide ir al concierto con Carlos.

Viewing

2. Match the dialogues with their corresponding pictures.

   1. _____   2. _____   3. _____

   a. — Tengo muchas ganas de ir a la fiesta. Lo siento, Carlos.
   — Bueno. Podemos ir juntos a la fiesta entonces.

   b. — ¡Aquí estamos!
   — Ay, lo siento mucho... es que Hiroshi no llega hasta el lunes.

   c. — ¿Vienes a la fiesta?
   — Sí, claro. Me gustaría mucho.

3. Circle all of the phrases that describe Hiroshi.

es estudiante	es de San Francisco	tiene 17 años
es de Japón	tiene 16 años	va a vivir en Quito

Post-viewing

4. Put the following events in the correct order.

   _____ **a.** María se pone una chaqueta y se peina.

   _____ **b.** Carlos y Tomás llegan a la casa de María.

   _____ **c.** Los tres amigos hablan de Hiroshi.

   _____ **d.** Van a un café y toman jugo.

   _____ **e.** María dice que la fiesta es el próximo fin de semana.

CAPÍTULO 7

Activity Master 3

Panorama cultural

Supplementary Vocabulary		
los enamorados *people in love*	llamar la atención *to draw attention*	tropezar *to trip*
el/la extranjero,-a *foreigner*	la plática *conversation*	la vergüenza *embarrassment*

Viewing

1. Match each of the students interviewed with the way he or she usually meets people.

   _____ 1. Rodrigo   **a.** Busco una persona amiga mía que me la presente.

   _____ 2. Jessica   **b.** Le pido su número telefónico.

   _____ 3. María Isabel   **c.** Trato de tener conversación con él.

2. Match the student with his or her way of meeting someone.

   _____ 1. María Luisa   **a.** Converso con él y veo si es que realmente me gusta o no.

   _____ 2. Manolo   **b.** Le pregunto cualquier cosa para llamar la atención.

   _____ 3. Siria   **c.** Hago como que me tropiezo... y digo, ¡Ay!, perdón.

   _____ 4. Ixchel   **d.** Primero le pregunto su nombre... cuál es su edad....

   _____ 5. Carlos   **e.** Si es extranjero, le enseño los lugares de Costa Rica.

3. Indicate who each student says pays for a date by checking the appropriate box.

	el chico	la chica	los dos
Rodrigo			
Jessica			
María Isabel			
Ixchel			
Carlos			

Videoclips

Supplementary Vocabulary	
anda por Magaly *go get Magaly*	comunica con el mundo *puts you in touch with*
llamamos a saludarte *we called to say hi*	*the world*
la llamada de larga distancia nacional *national long distance call*	el 50 por ciento de descuento *50% discount*

Viewing

4. During what times of the day does the discount apply? Circle the correct answer.
   a. de 7:00 A.M. a 10:00 P.M.   **b.** de 7:00 P.M. a 7:00 A.M.   **c.** de 7:00 A.M. a 7:00 P.M.

5. What is EDA's slogan? Circle the correct answer.
   a. En Antioquia es rico vivir.
   b. Comunica a los antioqueños con el mundo.
   c. EDA le regala el cincuenta por ciento de descuento.

¡A comer!

Functions modeled in video:

DVD2 The DVD Tutor provides instant access to any part of the video program as well as the ability to repeat short segments as needed. The DVD Tutor also allows access to Spanish-language captions for all video segments as well as to video-based comprehension activities to assess student comprehension.

- talking about meals and food
- commenting on food
- making polite requests
- ordering dinner in a restaurant
- asking for and paying the bill in a restaurant

Video Segment	Correlation to Print Materials			Videocassette 3		Videocassette 5 (captioned)	
	Pupil's Edition	Video Guide		Start Time	Length	Start Time	Length
		Activity Masters	Scripts				
De antemano	pp. 232–233	p. 56	p. 102	18:10	6:19	1:17:46	6:19
A continuación		p. 57	pp. 102–103	24:30	6:15	1:24:07	6:19
Panorama cultural	p. 239*	p. 58	p. 103	31:02	3:54		
Videoclips		p. 58	pp. 103–104	34:58	1:46		

Video Synopses

De antemano ¿Qué vas a pedir?

María, her brother Roberto, and Tomás take Hiroshi to a restaurant that serves typical Ecuadorean dishes. They describe the food to Hiroshi, who decides to order **sancocho**. After eating and paying the bill, they set off for Otavalo. On their way they suddenly have car trouble.

¿Qué vas a pedir? (a continuación)

The characters are helped by a passerby and are soon on their way to Otavalo. While at the Otavalo open-air market, they buy traditional sweaters and gifts for Hiroshi and his family, as well as various other items. They return to Quito and recount the trip to Roberto and María's mother.

Panorama cultural ¿Cuál es un plato típico de tu país?

- Three teenagers from Florida, Venezuela, and Ecuador tell us about typical dishes from the regions where they live.

- In additional interviews, people from various Spanish-speaking countries tell us about dishes typical to their regions.

Videoclips

- **Leche Ram®:** advertisement for milk
- **Néctares Dos Pinos®:** advertisement for juice
- **La Casera®:** advertisement for bottled water

The DVD Tutor contains all video material plus video-based activities to assess student comprehension of **De antemano, A continuación,** and **Panorama cultural.** Short video segments are automatically replayed to prompt students if they answer incorrectly.

De antemano ¿Qué vas a pedir?

Pre-viewing
- Ask students at what time they usually eat lunch and what they usually have. Find out what students like to order when they go out to eat in a restaurant.

- Ask students to think about what words and phrases they usually say or hear when they are in a restaurant. Suggest that they watch for instances where video characters say these things to one another.

Viewing
- Tell students that Quito is located in the Andes region. Have students listen for the Andean flute music which accompanies the video. Tell them that some musical instruments of the region include **la quena** (native South American notched flute), **la zampoña** (panpipe), and **el rondador** (Ecuadorean panpipe).

- Pause the video at the closeup of **locro** and have students list the ingredients in it.

- Have students pay close attention to the scene in which Roberto pays the bill and ask them how much the meal costs.

Post-viewing
- Ask students at what time the video characters ate. Mention the fact that in many Spanish-speaking countries lunch is served around 2:00 P.M. and is usually the biggest meal of the day.

- You might want to have students research **locro, sancocho, ají,** or other Ecuadorean dishes and describe to the rest of the class what kind of ingredients go into making them.

- Have students calculate a reasonable tip for the waiter.

¿Qué vas a pedir? (a continuación)

Pre-viewing
- Have students locate Ecuador on a map and identify the equator. Explain to students that monuments to the equator can be found across the globe, and in Ecuador the small structure and long promenade marking 0° latitude are located near San Antonio de Pichincha, fifteen miles north of Quito.

- Ask students if they have ever shopped in an open-air market or purchased anything by bargaining. Discuss the advantages and disadvantages of bargaining.

Viewing
- Show the video without sound and ask students what the teenagers in the video are wearing. What is the weather like? What type of vegetation and geographical features do they notice? Why is Hiroshi buying a sweater at the equator? How do they think the altitude of the mountains affects the climate and plant life growing in this region of Equador?

- Show the video with sound and ask students to write the prices mentioned during the bargaining sessions. Then have students calculate how much María saved by bargaining. (ten dollars)

Post-viewing
- Ask students how the prices for the meal and the gifts Hiroshi buys compare to those for the same items in the United States. Tell students that the currency of Equador used to be the **sucre.** Have students research the history of the exchange rate of the **sucre** before its alignment with the dollar and how the alignment affected the Equadorian economy.

- Have students role-play a scene in which they try to bargain with a salesperson over a particular item. You may wish to replay the scene in which María bargains with the man at the market.

Spanish 1 ¡Ven conmigo!

Panorama cultural

Pre-viewing

- Ask students if they have tried foods from other countries or other regions within the United States. If so, what kinds?

- Students who are native speakers may want to answer the question, ¿Cuál es un plato típico de tu país? You might ask if they want to describe a dish typical of their family's place of origin and list its main ingredients.

Viewing

- Ask students what the typical dishes from Miami and Venezuela have in common. (arroz)

- Ask students what Sra. González from Spain and Ema from Mexico both say forms part of a typical dish in their country. Then, point out that the tortilla in Spain is an egg omelet, but in Mexico the tortilla is a thin, round, unleavened bread.

- The first Panorama cultural activity on Activity Master 3 is based on the first three interviews only.

Post-viewing

- Ask students what Gisela says is a typical dish in Venezuela. Discuss with them the idea that having many different kinds of food available makes the idea of a typical dish obsolete. Ask what are the advantages and disadvantages of everyone eating the same kinds of foods.

- Have students create a menu in which they list all the dishes mentioned in the interviews as well as other typical dishes from Spanish-speaking countries.

Videoclips

- Ask students to describe a few beverage commercials they have seen on TV. Have them identify the type of beverage being advertised, the age group being targeted, and the advertising strategies used to sell the product.

- Show the videoclips once without sound. Ask students to guess the type of beverage being advertised in each of the three videoclips (milk, fruit juice, water), and the brand names used. (Ram®, Dos Pinos®, La Casera®)

- Play the videoclips with sound and ask students to listen for the following words: leche, néctares, and La Casera®. They might want to tally the times they hear each one. (leche–2, néctares–1, La Casera®–6)

- Ask students which of the three commercials they like the most, and why.

Colorín colorado

Have students work in groups and role-play a restaurant scene in which they order food and pay the bill. Students should ask for a recommendation from the waitperson, as well as a description of the food from the others at the table. You may want to use the menus that students made as a Panorama cultural Post-viewing activity suggestion.

Activity Master 1

De antemano ¿Qué vas a pedir?

Supplementary Vocabulary	
el chile *chile pepper*	la empanada *meat turnover*
el condimento *condiment*	las verduras *vegetables*

Viewing

1. Indicate what each person orders.

   a. empanadas   **c.** carne colorada   **e.** jugo de naranja
   b. sancocho   **d.** locro   **f.** agua

	1. Tomás	2. María	3. Roberto	4. Hiroshi
food	_____	_____	_____	_____
drink	_____	_____	_____	_____

2. According to Tomás's description, which of the following is **ají?** Circle the correct letter.

   a.   b.

3. Look at the pictures in Activity 2 and decide which of the following ingredients would be used in each. Write the letter of each corresponding photo next to each ingredient.

   papas _____   chiles _____
   cebollas _____   tomate _____
   aguacate _____   queso _____

Post-viewing

4. What kinds of foods commonly eaten in the United States are similar to **locro** and **ají?**

   locro: _____

   ají: _____

5. Circle the best answer to the following questions.

   1. ¿Por qué a Hiroshi no le gusta el ají?

      a. Está muy picante.   **b.** Está muy caliente.

   2. ¿Por que no pide empanadas Tomás?

      a. El restaurante no tiene empanadas.   **b.** No le gustan las empanadas.

   3. ¿Qué tipo de comida sirve el restaurante?

      a. comida china muy buena   **b.** platos típicos de la región andina

Spanish 1 ¡Ven conmigo!

CAPÍTULO 8

Activity Master 2

¿Qué vas a pedir? (a continuación)

Supplementary Vocabulary		
la bufanda *scarf*	regatear *to bargain*	el tanque *tank*
la emergencia *emergency*	sabroso/a *tasty*	el tapiz *rug*
la gasolina *gasoline*	el suéter de lana *wool sweater*	

Pre-viewing

1. Make a list of six items you might be able to find at an open-air market.

   _____   _____   _____

   _____   _____   _____

Viewing

2. Indicate the original price the vendor quoted for each of the following items and the amount the video characters ended up paying. Write the letter of the correct price in the blank space.

   a. $30.00   **c.** $15.00   **e.** $20.00
   b. $25.00   **d.** $12.00   **f.** $18.00

                  original price   final price

   1. tapiz   _____   _____

   2. suéter de lana   _____   _____

Post-viewing

3. Put the following events in the correct order.

   _____ **a.** Los muchachos van a Mitad del Mundo.

   _____ **b.** Tomás admira el tapiz y la bufanda.

   _____ **c.** Un hombre les da gasolina a los jóvenes.

   _____ **d.** María compra un tapiz para Hiroshi.

   _____ **e.** Hiroshi compra un suéter para su hermana.

4. With a partner, follow the directions to create a dialogue between Hiroshi and a vendor selling sweaters.

Hiroshi
1. Greet the vendor.
2. Ask how much the sweater is.
3. Tell him the price is a little high and offer a lower price.
4. Offer a price higher than your original price but lower than his final offer.
5. Agree on the price and thank him.

Vendor
1. Greet your customer.
2. Tell your customer a price for the sweater.
3. Give him a final offer lower than your original price but higher than his offer.
4. Agree on the price slightly lower than your final offer.
5. Thank him and say goodbye.

CAPÍTULO 8

Activity Master 3

Panorama cultural

Supplementary Vocabulary

el ajo *garlic*	el gazpacho *cold tomato-based soup*
la caraota *black bean*	la masa *dough*
carne mechada y tajada *shredded meat and plantain*	los mineros *mine workers*
el chancho *pork*	el mole *Mexican sauce made with chile peppers and chocolate*
empanizado/a *breaded*	el pimiento *bell pepper*
el gandule *pigeon pea*	la yuca *cassava root*

Viewing

1. Match the person being interviewed with a typical dish of his or her country or region.

1. _____   2. _____   3. _____

    a. el pabellón
    b. huevos fritos con llapingachos y lechuga
    c. plátanos maduros con bistec empanizado

2. Match the **plato típico** with its ingredients.

_____ **1.** el pabellón   **a.** pollo, papa, maíz

_____ **2.** llapingachos   **b.** masa, arroz, chancho

_____ **3.** ajiaco colombiano   **c.** arroz, caraotas, carne mechada y tajada

_____ **4.** enchiladas   **d.** tortilla, pollo, queso, crema, verduras, salsa

_____ **5.** nacatamales   **e.** tortillas de papa, queso

Videoclips

Supplementary Vocabulary

energía inagotable *renewable energy*	han descubierto *have discovered*	sin ella *without it*
enriquecido/a *enriched*	hombre a borda *man overboard*	verdadero sabor *real flavor*
estos angelitos *these little angels*	saber *to have flavor*	vitaminado/a *with added vitamins*

3. Write **a**, **b**, or **c** next to each phrase, according to which commercial you hear the phrase in.

    a. Leche Ram®   **b.** Néctares Dos Pinos®   **c.** La Casera®

_____ **1.** ¡Sí, sabes!

_____ **2.** ... enriquecida con vitaminas.

_____ **3.** Rápido, comida para este hombre.

4. Complete each slogan below by writing the name of the product in the blank space.

1. _____ No coma sin ella.

2. _____ Energía inagotable.

3. _____ Verdadero sabor.

CAPÍTULO 8

Location: Texas

DVD Tutor, Disc 2
Videocassette 3
Start Time: 36:59
Length: 2:09
Pupil's Edition pp. 260–263

The Spanish in the Location Opener is spoken at a normal speed. Students are not expected to understand everything. The activities for this section have been designed to help them understand the major points.

 Teaching Suggestions

 The DVD Tutor contains all video material plus a video-based activity to assess student comprehension after viewing the Location Opener. Short segments are automatically replayed to prompt students if they answer incorrectly.

Pre-viewing

- Have students locate Texas on the map of the United States on p. xxix of the *Pupil's Edition*. Ask students which state in the United States has the longest border with Mexico. (Texas) Ask students if they believe Mexico is west of Texas at any point, rather than south of it. (For over half the latitude of the state, parts of Mexico are west of Texas.)

- Students may use the map of Texas on p. 261 of the *Pupil's Edition* to look for Spanish place names (cities, rivers, mountains, islands, etc.). Have them find **El Paso**, **el río Guadalupe**, **la Isla del Padre**, and **San Antonio**, in particular, as they will hear these names in the video segment.

- Tell students that although about 12% of the total U.S. population is Hispanic, over 30% of Texans are Hispanic. In several cities, such as San Antonio, over half of the population is Hispanic. Most Hispanic people in Texas are Mexican Americans. Ask students how they think Texan culture might be different from cultures in other parts of the United States as a result of Mexican Americans' contributions. They should think of specific aspects of daily life, such as food, music, language, architecture, pastimes, and so on.

- Explain to students that after Mexico won its independence from Spain in 1821, Texas remained part of Mexico. Sieur de la Salle of France founded Fort Saint Louis in 1682 on the coast of Texas. In 1836, Texas became an independent nation, called the Republic of Texas. The Republic ended in 1845, when Texas was admitted to the United States as the 28th state. Ask students how many governments have ruled Texas. (Six: Spain, France, Mexico, Republic of Texas, Confederate States of America, United States)

Viewing

- Play the video without sound and have students list geographical or man-made features shown in the video. (mesa, canyon, river, beach, mission, market) Then play the video with sound and have them write the names of places as they hear them. (**la misión de San José**, **San Antonio**, **El Paso**, **el río Guadalupe**, **la Isla del Padre**, **el Paseo del Río**, **la Plaza del Mercado**)

- Play the video with sound. Ask students to make a list of things they see in the video which show a blending of cultures. (Answers will vary, but possible examples are the guitar, Mexican American food items, and San Antonio's **Plaza del Mercado**.)

- Play the video again with sound and have students complete Activities 1 and 2 on Activity Master, p. 60. You may need to play the video more than once.

Post-viewing

Ask students to name the things that they associate with Texas (in Spanish, if possible). Write them on the board or on a transparency. Then ask students which of those things they knew about or expected to be true before viewing the video. Erase those items, leaving only the ones that students learned about from the video or found to be surprising.

Activity Master: Location Opener

Supplementary Vocabulary

la herencia mexicana *Mexican heritage*

más de la mitad de la población *more than half the population*

millones de visitantes *millions of visitors*

el segundo estado más grande y más poblado *the second biggest and most populated state*

seis banderas han ondeado sobre Texas *six flags have flown over Texas*

su aire mexicano *its Mexican air, atmosphere*

la vida colonial española de hace doscientos años *colonial life 200 years ago*

Viewing

1. Place a check mark next to the things you see in the video. Some items do not appear in the video.

   _____ **a.** la misión de San José   _____ **g.** San Antonio

   _____ **b.** la nieve   _____ **h.** una familia en el campo

   _____ **c.** los mariachis   _____ **i.** la capital de Texas

   _____ **d.** el río Guadalupe   _____ **j.** un barco turístico en el río

   _____ **e.** la Isla del Padre   _____ **k.** el Paseo del Río con cafés al aire libre

   _____ **f.** las comidas, la música, las fiestas   _____ **l.** la Plaza del Mercado con tiendas y restaurantes

Post-viewing

2. Based on what you learned from the video, place a check mark next to the best caption for the picture.

   _____ **a.** Texas abarca grandes comunidades francesas y alemanas.

   _____ **b.** El pasado hispano de Texas vive aún en los nombres como San Antonio y El Paso.

   _____ **c.** La mayoría de los hispanohablantes en Texas son cubanos.

   _____ **d.** Más de la mitad de la población de Texas es méxicoamericana.

Spanish 1 ¡Ven conmigo!

¡Vamos de compras!

Functions modeled in video:

 The DVD Tutor provides instant access to any part of the video program as well as the ability to repeat short segments as needed. The DVD Tutor also allows access to Spanish-language captions for all video segments as well as to video-based comprehension activities to assess student comprehension.

- discussing gift suggestions
- asking for and giving directions downtown
- commenting on clothes
- making comparisons
- expressing preferences
- asking about prices and paying for something

Video Segment	Correlation to Print Materials			Videocassette 3		Videocassette 5 (captioned)	
	Pupil's Edition	Video Guide		Start Time	Length	Start Time	Length
		Activity Masters	Scripts				
De antemano	pp. 266–267	p. 64	p. 104	39:08	4:00	1:30:27	4:00
A continuación		p. 65	p. 105	43:09	4:09	1:34:29	4:11
Panorama cultural	p. 273*	p. 66	pp. 105–106	47:18	3.23		
Videoclips		p. 66	p. 106	50:42	0:46		

 ## Video Synopses

De antemano ¿Qué le compramos a Héctor?

Eva, Lisa, and Gabi go shopping for graduation presents for Héctor. They take a few moments to look at some clothing for themselves. Finally they decide to split up and shop separately and meet back together in half an hour. Without knowing, each of the girls buys Héctor exactly the same poster as a gift.

¿Qué le compramos a Héctor? (a continuación)

When Eva, Lisa, and Gabi get back together, they walk around San Antonio and listen to a **mariachi** band. When they realize that they all have the same gift, Eva and Gabi decide to return theirs for a CD and a different poster.

Panorama cultural ¿Estás a la moda?

- Native speakers from Spain, Venezuela, and Costa Rica tell us about what they think is in style and what is not.
- In additional interviews, people from various Spanish-speaking countries tell us their opinions about fashion.

Videoclips

2 X 1: advertisement for a department store

Teaching Suggestions

The DVD Tutor contains all video material plus video-based activities to assess student comprehension of **De antemano, A continuación,** and **Panorama cultural.** Short video segments are automatically replayed to prompt students if they answer incorrectly.

CAPÍTULO 9

De antemano ¿Qué le compramos a Héctor?

Pre-viewing

- Have students locate San Antonio on the map on p. 261 of the *Pupil's Edition*. Point out that Texas was part of Mexico until its independence in 1836, and eventually became a U.S. state in 1845. Tell students that more than half of the population of San Antonio is of Hispanic origin. Spanish is not only widely spoken, but there are also Spanish-language newspapers, radio, and television programs in San Antonio.

- Take a poll of how many students do or do not like to go shopping. Then ask students to brainstorm for reasons to go shopping.

- Ask students what they think are common graduation gifts for a male friend. Suggest that they listen for gift ideas as they watch the video.

Viewing

- Ask students to listen for the purpose of the girls' shopping trip. (to buy Héctor a graduation gift)

- Have students write the names of the different kinds of shops mentioned in the video. (**papelería, librería, zapatería**) Point out that the Spanish words for all these specialized stores end in -**ería.**

Post-viewing

- Ask students what they think of the present the video characters chose for Héctor. Would they like to receive something like that? What would they have chosen for Héctor?

- Have students work in pairs and write a conversation in which they discuss buying a gift for a friend. Have them discuss what they are going to buy and where they will go to buy it. Then ask for volunteers to present the dialogue to the class.

¿Qué le compramos a Héctor? (a continuación)

Pre-viewing

Ask students if they have ever heard street musicians where they live. Explain to them that in San Antonio it is not unusual to see **mariachi** bands—groups of musicians who play the violin, the guitar, the trumpet, and other instruments, and sing traditional Mexican songs—play in restaurants or in tourist spots such as **el Paseo del Río.**

Viewing

- Have students watch the scene in which Gabi dances with the **mariachi.** Ask students if there are any traditional dances that they know of which are similar. (square dancing)

- Have students watch for the resolution of the gift dilemma. How did the girls settle the problem? Who will give Héctor the poster? What will the others give him? (Lisa will give him the poster, Eva will give him a CD, and Gabi will give him a different poster.)

Post-viewing

- Have students do research projects on **mariachi** bands, San Antonio, Mexican folk dancing, or other Mexican American traditions.

- Enrich students' experience of **mariachi** music by playing authentic recordings in class.

Spanish 1 ¡Ven conmigo!

Panorama cultural

Pre-viewing
- Discuss fashion trends with students and how style has changed throughout the decades. Use the chart on Activity Master 3, p. 66, to take a poll of students' opinions on style. How many think that it is important to be fashionable and how many do not? Is it important all of the time? When is it not?
- Ask students if they think that other countries' fashions are the same or different from those in the United States.

Viewing
- Ask students to keep count of how many students feel that being in style is important and how many do not.
- Ask students to discuss why Rodrigo and Johnny might be considered opposites when it comes to their opinions on style.
- Activity 2 on Activity Master 3 is based on the first three interviews only.

Post-viewing
Have students compare the results of the fashion poll they took in class with the opinions of the people interviewed in the video. Does the class feel that style is less important or more important than the interviewees?

Videoclips

- Tell students they are going to see an ad for a department store in a Latin American country. Ask students what they think it might look like.
- Play the videoclip once without sound and ask students to look for clues that the store in the videoclip is in a Spanish-speaking country. (They may be surprised how similar the store is to any they may have near home.)
- Play the videoclip with sound. Ask students to listen for the name of the store and the country it is in. (2 X 1 (“**dos por uno**”), Costa Rica) Ask if students can translate the name of the store into English. (Two for One) Do they think this is a good name for the department store? Why or why not?

Colorín colorado

Use the **Panorama cultural** interviews as a resource for students to write a **De moda** advice column for teens in their school. Have them put the opinions of the interviewees in their column, as well as those of fellow students.

Activity Master 1

De antemano ¿Qué le compramos a Héctor?

Supplementary Vocabulary	
devolver *to return*	la papelería *stationery store*

Pre-viewing

1. What would you give your best friend as a graduation gift? Write three possible gift items in Spanish.

   _____   _____   _____

Viewing

2. Place a check mark next to the items Eva, Gabi, and Lisa look at when they're shopping.

   _____ **a.** una blusa roja   _____ **e.** unos pantalones cortos de cuadros

   _____ **b.** un vestido blanco   _____ **f.** unos zapatos

   _____ **c.** una blusa de rayas   _____ **g.** una falda

   _____ **d.** unos carteles   _____ **h.** una corbata negra

3. Number the pictures in the correct order.

   _____ **a.** Gabi   _____ **b.** Eva   _____ **c.** Lisa

Post-viewing

4. Write **C** for **cierto** or **F** for **falso** next to each item.

   _____ **1.** Eva, Gabi y Lisa quieren comprar un regalo divertido.

   _____ **2.** A Gabi no le gustan los pantalones cortos.

   _____ **3.** Lisa compra una falda de algodón.

   _____ **4.** Las tres amigas le compran a Héctor un disco compacto de Gloria Estefan.

   _____ **5.** Las amigas pasan dos horas en buscar algo para Héctor.

   _____ **6.** Las chicas van de compras en un centro comercial.

5. Rewrite the false sentences in Activity 4 so that they're true.

   _____

   _____

   _____

   _____

Spanish 1 ¡Ven conmigo!

Activity Master 2

¿Qué le compramos a Héctor? (a continuación)

> **Supplementary Vocabulary**
> el amatista *amethyst*   la plata *silver*
> el anillo *ring*   precioso/a *beautiful*

Pre-viewing

1. Which item did all three girls buy for Héctor? Circle the correct answer.

un disco compacto   un cartel

una camiseta   unos pantalones cortos

Viewing

2. Indicate who says the following statements by writing **E** for Eva, **L** for Lisa, or **G** for Gabi.

_____ 1. ¿Por qué no vamos a la nueva joyería?

_____ 2. Yo prefiero el anillo de plata.

_____ 3. ¿Sabe usted por qué están aquí los mariachis?

_____ 4. Ay, Gabi, tenemos el mismo cartel.

_____ 5. Hay otro cartel que me gusta en la misma tienda.

Eva   **Lisa**   **Gabi**

Post-viewing

3. Indicate the order in which the following scenes take place by numbering the pictures in the correct order. Then, draw a line to match each picture with the appropriate statement.

_____

a. Ay, yo también tengo un cartel para Héctor.

_____

b. ¡Ese anillo es precioso!

_____

c. Debe ser un grupo de los que están aquí para el festival.

Activity Master 3

Panorama cultural

Supplementary Vocabulary		
los años sesenta *the 60s*	fino/a *formal*	quedarse atrás *to stay behind*
ajustado/a *tight*	lo adecuado *what is appropriate*	suecos *clogs*
andar en la actualidad *to be current*	los lugares nocturnos *night spots*	vestirse *to dress*
la boda *wedding*	la manga *sleeve*	
los borceguíes *boots*	uno mismo/a *oneself*	

Pre-viewing

1. Use the following chart to interview three classmates about the importance of style.

En tu opinión, ¿es importante la moda?

Nombre	nunca		a veces		siempre	
1.	0	1	2	3	4	5
2.	0	1	2	3	4	5
3.	0	1	2	3	4	5

Viewing

2. Place a check mark next to the clothing items that are mentioned in the interviews.

_____ **a.** vestido   _____ **d.** zapatillas de tenis

_____ **b.** traje de baño   _____ **e.** bluejeans

_____ **c.** ropa de sport   _____ **f.** traje

3. Place a check mark next to the names of the people who feel that being fashionable is important.

_____ **1.** Soledad   _____ **5.** Rodrigo   _____ **9.** Gala

_____ **2.** Gisela   _____ **6.** Gretel   _____ **10.** Jaharlyn

_____ **3.** Pablo   _____ **7.** Cindy

_____ **4.** Yaremi   _____ **8.** Johnny

Videoclips

Supplementary Vocabulary	
acogedor,-a *cozy*	personal amable *friendly staff*
los intermediarios *middlemen*	sale ganando *you come out a winner*
justo/a *fair*	la tienda de departamentos *department store*
pasillos amplios *wide aisles*	verdadero/a *real, genuine*

Viewing

4. Place a check mark next to the phrases you hear spoken in the videoclip.

_____ **a.** empleados simpáticos   _____ **d.** precios baratos

_____ **b.** personal amable   _____ **e.** usted siempre sale con una ganga

_____ **c.** precios justos   _____ **f.** usted siempre sale ganando

CAPÍTULO 9

Celebraciones

Functions modeled in video:

The DVD Tutor provides instant access to any part of the video program as well as the ability to repeat short segments as needed. The DVD Tutor also allows access to Spanish-language captions for all video segments as well as to video-based comprehension activities to assess student comprehension.

- talking about what you're doing right now
- asking for and giving an opinion
- asking for help and responding to requests
- telling a friend what to do
- talking about past events

Video Segment	Correlation to Print Materials			Videocassette 4		Videocassette 5 (captioned)	
	Pupil's Edition	Video Guide		Start Time	Length	Start Time	Length
		Activity Masters	Scripts				
De antemano	pp. 294–295	p. 70	p. 106	1:15	4:06	1:38:41	4:06
A continuación		p. 71	pp. 106–107	5:22	5:32	1:42:48	5:35
Panorama cultural	p. 301*	p. 72	pp. 107–108	11:17	3:42		
Videoclips		p. 72	p. 108	15:02	0:36		

 Video Synopses

De antemano ¡Felicidades Héctor!

The Villarreal family is making preparations for Héctor's graduation party. While making **tamales**, Héctor's grandmother tells Lisa, Eva, and Gabi about holidays in Mexico. At the end of the episode, Héctor's father discovers that he has forgotten to send out the invitations to the party which is set to begin in two hours.

¡Felicidades Héctor! (a continuación)

Hector's mother calls all of the guests on the telephone and invites them to the party. Eva, Lisa, and Gabi go to the bakery to pick up the cake and mistakenly bring back the wrong one. Fortunately, they have just enough time to exchange the cake and return before Héctor gets home. In the end, the party is a success.

Panorama cultural ¿Qué hacen ustedes para celebrar?

- Spanish-speaking people from Texas, Spain, and Venezuela tell us about holidays and celebrations where they live.
- In additional interviews, people from various Spanish-speaking countries tell us about their favorite celebrations and holidays.

Videoclips

IDEA: public service announcement concerning Christmas holidays

Spanish 1 ¡Ven conmigo!

Video Guide **67**

The DVD Tutor contains all video material plus video-based activities to assess student comprehension of **De antemano, A continuación,** and **Panorama cultural.** Short video segments are automatically replayed to prompt students if they answer incorrectly.

De antemano ¡Felicidades Héctor!

Pre-viewing
- Ask students if they have ever given a surprise party for someone. What preparations had to be made? What foods did they serve? Who helped with the preparations?
- Have the class make a "To Do" list of what they would need to buy and do in order to have a party. Write responses on the board or on a transparency and provide appropriate Spanish expressions when necessary.

Viewing
- Have students make a list of the family members who are helping prepare for the party and write what each member's task is.
- Play the scene in which Héctor's father calls the bakery. Have students imagine they are the bakery employee and fill out the order form in Activity 1 on Activity Master 1, p. 70.
- Have students make a list of the holidays mentioned by Héctor's grandmother.

Post-viewing
- Ask students what dish was being prepared especially for Héctor, and when it would usually be eaten. Explain to students that a **tamal** is a dish made of cornmeal, meat, and vegetables, and wrapped in corn husks or banana leaves. Ask students who are native speakers what special holiday foods are part of their families' holiday traditions.
- Have students review the list of holidays mentioned by Héctor's grandmother. Have them choose one and prepare a short presentation on specific traditions associated with that holiday.

¡Felicidades Héctor! (a continuación)

Pre-viewing
Ask students what they would do if they found out that they had forgotten to mail invitations to a party that was going to start in about two hours. Ask them to predict what Héctor's mother will do when she learns of the mistake.

Viewing
- Have students pick out the three dilemmas which take place before Héctor's party. (invitations not mailed, wrong cake, Héctor on his way home too early)
- Ask students what was wrong with the first cake and what was written on it. (**Felices Quince Años Angela**) Explain to students the concept of the **fiesta de quinceañera.** Point out that it is a special birthday party for girls who turn fifteen. In many Hispanic regions, the occasion is celebrated with a mass followed by a large party.

Post-viewing
- Discuss the resolution of the party invitation disaster. Had students predicted it accurately? Do students think that such a solution would work, or did they have better solutions?
- Ask students why they think Héctor's parents say that everything went well and that they didn't have any problems in preparing for the party. Were they being serious or sarcastic?

Spanish 1 ¡Ven conmigo!

CAPÍTULO 10

Panorama cultural

Pre-viewing
- Have students name several U.S. holidays that they would describe to a visitor from another country. How would they describe them?
- Discuss with students different ways of celebrating holidays such as parades, music, dancing, special foods, etc.

Viewing
- Have students make a list of all the celebrations that are mentioned in the interviews. Then, have them listen again and write the dates of the celebrations. Not all interviewees give a date.
- See the note on the Battle of Carabobo in the *Annotated Teacher's Edition*, p. 301.
- **La batalla de Pichincha** refers to the final battle of independence that General José Antonio de Sucre fought against the Spanish army in 1822. The site of this battle is called today the **Cima de la Libertad**. It overlooks Quito, the capital of Ecuador.
- The first **Panorama cultural** activity on Activity Master 3 is based on the first three interviews only.

Post-viewing
- Ask students how the holidays described in the interviews are similar to or different from U.S. holidays.
- Have students interview their classmates about different holidays by asking **¿Qué haces para celebrar ___?**
- Have students compare the celebration Claudia describes with Mardi Gras. Mardi Gras, which means "Fat Tuesday" in French, is a celebration held on Shrove Tuesday, the day before Lent begins. The Mardi Gras celebration in New Orleans is famous for its street parades, elaborate floats, marching bands, and outrageous costumes.

Videoclips

- Tell students that this videoclip is a public service message by the **Instituto para el Desarrollo de Antioquia (IDEA)**. Antioquia is a department in Colombia. Point out what **desarrollo** means. (development) Ask students what role they think IDEA plays. (working to improve quality of life for **antioqueños,** people from Antioquia)
- Ask students to close their eyes while you play the videoclip. Ask them to listen to the background music and guess what holiday it is. (Christmas)
- Ask students to name several occupations where people who do those jobs wouldn't be home for Christmas. (possible answers: medical personnel, fire fighters) Play the video and ask students to look for such people.

Colorín colorado

Replay the **Panorama cultural** interviews. Have students plan a class celebration around a specific holiday mentioned in the video. Have them discuss preparations which should include such activities as sending invitations, preparing special foods, decorations, music.

Activity Master 1

De antemano ¡Felicidades Héctor!

Supplementary Vocabulary		
felicidades *congratulations*	los fuegos artificiales *fireworks*	la tumba *tomb, grave*

Viewing

1. Fill out the following form with the information Héctor's father gives to the bakery over the phone.

> #27305
>
> Apellido: _____ Nombre: _____
>
> Tipo de pastel: _____ vainilla   _____ chocolate   _____ limón
>
> Mensaje: _____
>
> _____

2. Match the holidays with the traditions, according to what Héctor's grandmother says.

   _____ 1. la Navidad   **a.** desfiles

   _____ 2. el Día de la Independencia   **b.** tamales

   _____ 3. las Pascuas   **c.** visita a la tumba

   _____ 4. el Día de los Muertos   **d.** fuegos artificiales

Post-viewing

3. Match the person or group of persons with what they do to help prepare for the party.

   _____ 1. ayudar con las decoraciones   _____ 3. llamar a la pastelería

   _____ 2. preparar tamales   _____ 4. ir a la pastelería

   a. Tío Tomás, Tía Marcela y Juan   **b. Sr. Villarreal**   **c. Lisa y Gabi**

4. Circle the best answer for what happens at the end of the video episode.

   a. Manuel no prepara toda la comida que ellos necesitan para la fiesta.

   b. Héctor no puede venir a la fiesta porque no tiene una invitación.

   c. Manuel no manda las invitaciones a los invitados.

Spanish 1 ¡Ven conmigo!

Activity Master 2

¡Felicidades Héctor! (a continuación)

Supplementary Vocabulary
¡Qué lío! *What a mess!*
sospechar *to suspect*

Viewing

1. Place a check mark next to the sentences that describe Héctor.

_____ 1. Es su quinceañera.

_____ 2. Es su graduación.

_____ 3. Va a ir a UCLA.

_____ 4. Va a trabajar en San Antonio.

_____ 5. Sale para Los Ángeles en octubre.

_____ 6. Trabaja hasta las dos.

Post-viewing

2. Summarize what happened in *¡Felicidades Héctor!* *(a continuación)* by completing the sentences in the past tense with the verbs in the word bank and then numbering the sentences in the correct order.

llegar regresar llamar
mandar comprar

_____ **a.** Lisa, Eva y Gabi _____ el pastel.

_____ **b.** La señora Villarreal _____ a los invitados.

_____ **c.** Las chicas _____ a la pastelería.

_____ **d.** Héctor _____ a la fiesta.

_____ **e.** El señor Villarreal no _____ las invitaciones.

3. The following pictures represent the three problems that the Villarreals encounter during their preparations for Héctor's surprise party. Write three sentences in Spanish explaining what the problems are.

1.

2.

3.

1. _____

_____

2. _____

_____

3. _____

_____

CAPITULO 10

Activity Master 3

Panorama cultural

Supplementary Vocabulary

adornar las calles *to decorate the streets*	el carnaval *carnival, Mardi Gras*	la libertad *liberty*
la antorcha *torch*	la comparsa *street party*	rumbo a *towards (a destination)*
la asamblea *assembly*	el disfraz *costume*	
la bandera tricolor *three-colored flag*	inaugurar *to inaugurate*	

Viewing

1. Match each celebration with the sentence that describes it.

_____ 1. la fiesta de la Virgen del Rosario   **a.** Hay bailes típicos gallegos.

_____ 2. la batalla de Carabobo   **b.** Es el 16 de septiembre.

_____ 3. el Día de Independencia de México   **c.** Todos los militares salen a desfilar.

2. Indicate whether the following people describe a historical celebration or a religious celebration by writing **H** or **R** next to their names.

_____ 1. Sra. Pardo   _____ 5. Carlo Magno

_____ 2. Angélica   _____ 6. Ana María

_____ 3. Verónica   _____ 7. Elena y Blanca

_____ 4. Claudia   _____ 8. Ignacio

Post-viewing

3. Which holidays might you celebrate if you were in the following places on the dates indicated below?

_____ 1. Costa Rica, el 15 de septiembre   **a.** la Virgen del Sagrario

_____ 2. Texas, el 16 de septiembre   **b.** la Independencia de México

_____ 3. Ecuador, el 24 de mayo   **c.** la batalla de Pichincha

_____ 4. España, el 15 de agosto   **d.** la Independencia Patria

---

Videoclips

Supplementary Vocabulary

aunque no puedas estar *even though you can't be*

cierto que *it's true that*

Post-viewing

4. What is the message of the videoclip? Circle the letter of the best answer.

a. IDEA wishes everyone a merry Christmas, especially those that can't be with their loved ones.

b. IDEA warns everyone to drive carefully during the Christmas holidays.

c. IDEA thinks Christmas is a holiday you should spend at home.

CAPÍTULO 10

Location: Puerto Rico

DVD Tutor, Disc 2
Videocassette 4
Start Time: 15:52
Length: 2:21
Pupil's Edition pp. 322–325

The Spanish in the Location Opener is spoken at a normal speed. Students are not expected to understand everything. The activities for this section have been designed to help them understand the major points.

 Teaching Suggestions

 The DVD Tutor contains all video material plus a video-based activity to assess student comprehension after viewing the Location Opener. Short segments are automatically replayed to prompt students if they answer incorrectly.

Pre-viewing

- Have students list the things they associate with Caribbean islands. (palm trees, tropical flowers, beaches, rain forests, mountains, colorful buildings) Write the list on the board or on a transparency.

- Have students locate Puerto Rico on the map on p. xxvii of the *Pupil's Edition*. Have them locate San Juan—the capital and largest city—and Ponce, the second-largest city.

- Have students look at the photos on pp. 323–324 of the *Pupil's Edition*. Tell them to watch for some of the same scenes in the video.

- About three-fourths of Puerto Rico is mountainous. The **Cordillera Central** extends from the east coast to the west coast. The highest peak, **Cerro de Punta**, just north of Ponce, is about 1,338 m (4,400 ft.) high. Puerto Rico's tropical climate, with an annual mean temperature of 24°C (75°F), allows for a year-round growing season.

- The Caribbean National Forest (**Bosque Nacional del Caribe**), known popularly as **El Yunque**, is a 116-square-kilometer tropical rain forest preserve southeast of San Juan. In addition to the Location Opener segment, students will have a chance to see more of **El Yunque** in Chapter 12.

Viewing

- Play the video once without sound. Have students compare the list they made of things they associate with Caribbean islands to what they actually see in the video. Ask them how accurate their expectations were.

- Play the video with sound and ask students to listen for familiar words; for example, the names of Puerto Rico's two largest cities or the name of the rain forest preserve.

- Replay the video and have students complete Activities 1, 2, and 3 on Activity Master, p. 74. You may need to play the video more than once.

Post-viewing

- You may want students to work in small groups and use the images and information from the video to write a travel brochure telling about things to do in Puerto Rico.

- Have students research the rights and responsibilities of Puerto Ricans as U.S. citizens. (Puerto Ricans living on the mainland have all the rights and responsibilities of any other U.S. citizens. Puerto Ricans living in Puerto Rico may not vote in U.S. national elections and do not pay federal income tax.)

Activity Master: Location Opener

Supplementary Vocabulary

la belleza *beauty*	la isla de encantos *isle of enchantment*
el bosque *forest*	orgulloso/a *proud*
el destino turístico *tourist destination*	la Perla del Sur *Pearl of the South*
el edificio *building*	los ponceños *people from Ponce*
la fortaleza *fort*	el refugio *refuge*
hacer juego *to match (a color or design)*	el siglo dieciséis *16th century (the 1500s)*

Viewing

1. Match the name of each place on the left with its description on the right.

_____ 1. Puerto Rico   **a.** un bosque espectacular

_____ 2. San Juan   **b.** la Perla del Sur

_____ 3. El Yunque   **c.** una ciudad antigua, la capital

_____ 4. el Castillo San Felipe del Morro   **d.** una fortaleza construida en el siglo XVI

_____ 5. Ponce   **e.** isla de belleza y de encantos

Post-viewing

2. Complete each statement below with the correct word from the word bank.

> animales   playas   isla   capital

1. Puerto Rico, _____ de grandes bellezas naturales…

2. San Juan, su encantadora _____…

3. Hoy, San Juan es un importante destino turístico con sus monumentos históricos y

_____ atractivas.

4. El Yunque, un bosque espectacular, es el refugio de muchas especies de

_____ raros.

3. Based on what you've learned from the video, what do you think is shown in the picture? Circle the best answer.

a. El Yunque

b. El Morro

c. la Perla del Sur

d. playas atractivas

Spanish 1 ¡Ven conmigo!

11 Para vivir bien

Functions modeled in video:

 DVD2 The DVD Tutor provides instant access to any part of the video program as well as the ability to repeat short segments as needed. The DVD Tutor also allows access to Spanish-language captions for all video segments as well as to video-based comprehension activities to assess student comprehension.

- making suggestions and expressing feelings
- talking about moods and physical conditions
- saying what you did
- talking about where you went and when

Video Segment	Correlation to Print Materials			Videocassette 4		Videocassette 5 (captioned)	
	Pupil's Edition	Video Guide		Start Time	Length	Start Time	Length
		Activity Masters	Scripts				
De antemano	pp. 328–329	p. 78	pp. 108–109	18:12	7:33	1:48:24	7:32
A continuación		p. 79	pp. 109–110	25:47	6:52	1:55:57	6:56
Panorama cultural	p. 339*	p. 80	p. 110	32:39	3:03		
Videoclips		p. 80	p. 111	35:43	0:59		

 Video Synopses

De antemano *Un recorrido por San Juan*

Ben, Carmen, and their mother are New Yorkers visiting family in Puerto Rico. Ben and Carmen go sightseeing, but they need to meet their mother at 3:00 at **la Plaza de Hostos**. While resting on a park bench they meet Pedro, a boy from San Juan, who takes them on a tour of the city. After seeing **el Castillo del Morro**, Ben realizes that it is 2:55 and they have only five minutes to get to **la Plaza de Hostos**.

Un recorrido por San Juan (a continuación)

Ben, Carmen, and Pedro hurry to **la Plaza de Hostos** and make it in time to meet their mother. Ben and Carmen introduce Pedro to their mother, who realizes that Pedro is actually Ben and Carmen's cousin. Later that day they all go to watch Pedro, Ben, and Carmen's uncle play baseball.

Panorama cultural *¿Qué deporte practicas?*

- Teenagers from Mexico, Spain, and Florida tell us what sports they like to play and why.
- In additional interviews, people from various Spanish-speaking countries tell us about their favorite sports.

Videoclips

Happydent®: advertisement for sugarless chewing gum

Teaching Suggestions

The DVD Tutor contains all video material plus video-based activities to assess student comprehension of **De antemano, A continuación,** and **Panorama cultural.** Short video segments are automatically replayed to prompt students if they answer incorrectly.

De antemano *Un recorrido por San Juan*

Pre-viewing

- Ask students if they ever visit relatives or friends who live out of town. What kind of places do their relatives or friends show them while they are visiting?

- Ask students what places of interest would be appealing to visitors to their city or town.

- Tell students that the characters in the video will be describing how they feel after playing certain sports and activities. Suggest that students listen for the names of body parts as they watch the video. After you've played the episode, ask students if they could tell what body parts the characters talked about. (feet, nose, ears, lungs, heart)

Viewing

- Play the video without sound and have students look for clues that Puerto Rico is a Caribbean island. (palm trees, ocean)

- Have students list the places in San Juan that Carmen and Ben visit. Point out to students that Spanish influence is apparent in **el Viejo San Juan** where there are narrow cobblestone streets and colonial buildings, as well as at **El Morro**, a sixteenth-century Spanish fortress.

Post-viewing

- Have students create an imaginary walking tour in which they show someone around their city or town. Have them suggest things to do and places to see.

- Have students learn more about Puerto Rican family life by reading the children's book, *Yagua Days* by Cruz Martel. Students may create skits in Spanish based on the story.

Un recorrido por San Juan (a continuación)

Pre-viewing

- Ask students if they have family members that they have never met before. If so, what relation are they, and where do they live?

- Ask students what they think life would be like for a typical teenager on a tropical island like Puerto Rico. Would it be like a vacation in paradise? Then ask what they think life would be like in New York City.

Viewing

- Pause the video after Ben, Pedro, and Carmen buy drinks. Ask students to name three tropical fruits found in Puerto Rico. (**piña, guanábana, guineo**) Ask what fruit is **guineo**? (banana) Explain that the **guanábana** (soursop) is a fruit native to the Americas. Some people describe its taste as a mixture of pineapple and mango.

- Ask students how Ben and Pedro are related. (they are cousins) Who is Ben, Carmen, and Pedro's uncle? (tío Juan, a baseball player)

- Have students make two lists: one of things that they see at the stadium that is different from those at U.S. baseball games and one of things that is similar.

Post-viewing

Ask students to explain the misconceptions that Pedro has about New York City and those that Ben has about life in Puerto Rico. Were they similar to impressions that students expressed before viewing the video? In what ways?

CAPITULO 11

Panorama cultural

Pre-viewing

Ask students the question, **¿Qué deporte practicas?** and make a list on the board or on a transparency of all the sports played by students in the class. Ask if they think that teenagers in Spanish-speaking countries play the same sports.

Viewing

- Have students make a list of all of the sports mentioned by the people interviewed.
- Explain that **la charrería** is a Mexican rodeo-like competition. See the note about the **charro** costume in the *Annotated Teacher's Edition*, p. 77.
- Have students make a list of the English words that the Spanish speakers use to talk about different sports (**surf, softbol, soccer**). Point out that Spanish borrows many of its sports terms from English because of the fact that many sports originated in England or in the United States.
- The first **Panorama cultural** activity on Activity Master 3 is based on the first three interviews only.

Post-viewing

Have students compare the list of sports that they play with the list of sports the students in the video play. Which sports are in both lists? Which sports are unique to the United States and which ones are unique to Spanish-speaking countries?

Videoclips

- Play the videoclip and have students guess what the commercial is trying to sell. (sugarless gum)
- Replay the first commercial and ask students to look for the word that has been borrowed from another language. (happy) Ask students to name words used by U.S. products borrowed from other languages. (the cleanser Bon Ami® is an example)
- Pause the video when the **Happydent®** package is shown. Ask students to guess the flavor of the gum. (mint)
- Ask students how the commercial tries to persuade the viewer to use the product advertised. Do they think the commercial is successful?

Colorín colorado

Have students write a postcard to a friend in New York City from the perspective of either Ben or Carmen. They should explain where they went and what they did in Puerto Rico. You may want to have students design their own postcards with original art or pictures cut out of magazines.

Activity Master 1

De antemano *Un recorrido por San Juan*

Supplementary Vocabulary	
antiguo/a *old*	el edificio *building*
la banca *bench*	la palmera *palm tree*
el corazón *heart*	los pulmones *lungs*

Viewing

1. Place a check mark next to the parts of the body that are mentioned in the video.

_____ la cabeza _____ los pies _____ las orejas

_____ el corazón _____ los pulmones _____ el brazo

_____ la nariz _____ las piernas

2. Check the appropriate boxes to indicate the sport(s) each video character plays.

Ben				
Carmen				
Pedro				
el tío				

3. Match the following things with what the video characters say about them.

_____ 1. El Castillo del Morro   a. ¡Qué antiguo!

_____ 2. el ejercicio   b. Está contento.

_____ 3. el abuelo   c. Es bueno para los pulmones y el corazón.

_____ 4. Puerto Rico   d. Tiene edificios de muchos colores.

Post-viewing

4. Recreate Ben and Carmen's tour of San Juan by putting the following events in the correct order.

_____ a. Ben y Carmen van a la Plaza de Hostos.

_____ b. Visitan el Castillo del Morro.

_____ c. Conocen a Pedro.

_____ d. Le dicen adiós a su madre en la Plaza de Armas.

_____ e. Van a la Puerta de San Juan y al museo.

CAPÍTULO 11

Activity Master 2

Un recorrido por San Juan (a continuación)

┌───┐
│   **Supplementary Vocabulary**   │
│ la batida *milkshake*   el mundo es un pañuelo *it's a small world* │
│ la guanábana *soursop*   el rascacielos *skyscraper* │
│ el guineo *banana*   │
└───┘

Pre-viewing

1. Where did Ben and Carmen have to go at the end of the **De antemano** episode? Why?

     _____

     _____

Viewing

2. Choose the correct completion to each statement about Pedro's family.

    1. El padre de Pedro se llama _____.
       a. Juan Méndez   **b.** Pedro Méndez   **c.** Ricardo Méndez
    2. El apellido completo de Pedro es _____.
       a. Acevedo Méndez   **b.** Méndez Acevedo   **c.** Méndez Corredor
    3. La hermana de señora Corredor es la _____ de tío Juan.
       a. esposa   **b.** hermana   **c.** madre
    4. Carmen y Ben son los _____ de Pedro.
       a. primos   **b.** hermanos   **c.** tíos

Post-viewing

3. Look at the following pictures and number them in the correct order.

   a. _____   b. _____   c. _____   d. _____

4. Rewrite the following false statements in order to make them true.

    1. Carmen pide una batida de chocolate.

       _____

    2. La mamá de Carmen y Ben llega a la plaza temprano.

       _____

    3. En el barrio de Ben sólo hablan español.

       _____

    4. Pedro no va a la escuela.

       _____

    5. El tío Juan juega al fútbol en Nueva York.

CAPITULO 11

Activity Master 3

Panorama cultural

Supplementary Vocabulary		
las artes marciales *martial arts*	fortalecerse *to strengthen*	sudar *to sweat*
desahogarse *to relax*	el gasto *expense*	el surf *surfing*

Viewing

1. Draw a line from the name of the person to the sport he or she practices. Then draw a line from the sport to the reason why he or she practices it.

Víctor	el piragüismo	no es masculino
Manoli	la charrería	el agua me encanta
Raquel	el voleibol	por seguir la tradición

2. Write the name of the person under the picture of the sport(s) he or she plays.

Víctor   Paula   Shermine
Federico   José Antonio

1. _____

2. _____

3. _____

4. _____

5. _____

6. _____

3. Indicate if the following people like to play individual sports, team sports, or both, by writing **I** for **individual**, **E** for **equipo**, or **A** for **ambos** (*both*).

_____ 1. Víctor	_____ 5. Paula	_____ 9. Javier
_____ 2. Manoli	_____ 6. José Antonio	_____ 10. Jenny
_____ 3. Raquel	_____ 7. Shermine	_____ 11. Raúl
_____ 4. Federico	_____ 8. Rodrigo	

Videoclips

Post-viewing

4. Based on the videoclip, write **C** for **cierto** or **F** for **falso** next to each statement.

Supplementary Vocabulary
hace feliz *makes happy*
el chicle sin azúcar *sugarless gum*

_____ 1. Happydent® tiene azúcar.

_____ 2. Happydent® hace feliz a los dentistas.

_____ 3. El sabor de Happydent® es de fresa.

Las vacaciones ideales

Functions modeled in video:

The DVD Tutor provides instant access to any part of the video program as well as the ability to repeat short segments as needed. The DVD Tutor also allows access to Spanish-language captions for all video segments as well as to video-based comprehension activities to assess student comprehension.

- talking about what you do and like to do every day
- making future plans
- discussing what you would like to do on vacation
- saying where you went and what you did on vacation

Video Segment	Correlation to Print Materials			Videocassette 4		Videocassette 5 (captioned)	
	Pupil's Edition	Video Guide		Start Time	Length	Start Time	Length
		Activity Masters	Scripts				
De antemano	pp. 358–359	p. 84	p. 111	36:55	4:15	2:02:54	4:14
A continuación		p. 85	p. 111	41:10	6:18	2:07:09	6:18
Panorama cultural	p. 365*	p. 86	p. 112	47:46	2:14		
Videoclips		p. 86	p. 112	50:00	1:57		

Video Synopses

De antemano *Unas vacaciones ideales*

Ben and Carmen are bored, so their grandfather asks them what they would do on their ideal vacation. Ben says that he would travel down the Amazon in a canoe and explore the jungles of South America. Carmen says that she would sail the Pacific and find a deserted island. Then Ben and Carmen's mother comes in and tells them that they are going to take a short trip, but won't tell them where.

Unas vacaciones ideales (a continuación)

Ben and Carmen's mother surprises them by taking them to **El Yunque** National Park, where Ben finds an orchid and they hear a **coquí**. The next day they go to the beach for a picnic. With these two trips, Ben and Carmen feel they have ended up having their ideal vacations.

Panorama cultural *¿Adónde vas y qué haces en las vacaciones?*

- Teenagers from Argentina, Puerto Rico, and Venezuela talk what they do and where they go during their vacations.
- In additional interviews, people from various Spanish-speaking countries tell us about their vacations.

Videoclips

Los parques acuáticos: informational report about water parks in Spain

De antemano *Unas vacaciones ideales*

Pre-viewing

- Ask students if they have ever kept a journal. Do they think that it would be a good idea to keep a journal while on vacation? Why or why not?
- Ask students if they enjoy going on day trips. Have them make a list of three or more places nearby that they would like to visit. What would they do in each place?
- Tell students that in this episode, the characters describe a vacation they've just finished and mention what they'd like to do on a dream vacation. Ask students what expressions they might use to talk about these things. (**fuimos, visité, me gustaría, espero**) You might write them on the board and suggest that students listen for these or similar words as they watch the video.

Viewing

- Have students watch the opening scene, in which the Corredor family is at the beach, and make a list of what each of the family members is doing.
- Have students list the suggestions that **abuelo** gives to Ben and Carmen so that they won't be bored. Have them listen a second time and write the excuses the grandchildren give for not wanting to do what **abuelo** suggests.

Post-viewing

- Replay the Location Opener for Puerto Rico to show students some scenes of **El Yunque,** which Ben refers to in his journal.
- Discuss with students where they would go on a fantasy vacation. Ask them if Ben's or Carmen's ideal vacation sounds interesting. Why or why not?

Unas vacaciones ideales (a continuación)

Pre-viewing

- Ask students where they think Ben and Carmen might be going on their surprise trip.
- Point out to students that Puerto Rico not only has beautiful beaches, but also a rain forest called **El Yunque**. Rain forests, while they only cover about 6% of the Earth's total land surface, are home to about 75% of all known species of plants and animals.

Viewing

- **El Yunque** receives 240 inches, or 20 feet, of rainfall annually. Ask students how this compares to the annual rainfall in their region.
- Have students write the names of the animals and plants mentioned in the video. (**la cotorra, la boa, la orquídea, el coquí**) Point out that the **coquí** lives exclusively in Puerto Rico and is the only frog not born as a tadpole.

Post-viewing

Have students prepare short oral presentations on an animal or plant mentioned in the video, or any other species found in a tropical rainforest.

Panorama cultural

Pre-viewing
Discuss with students how much time they usually have off for vacation and what they usually do.

Viewing
- Ask students how much time off Jaharlyn has for vacation each year. (almost three months: two months in summer and three weeks at Christmas) Have students compare this with their school calendar.
- Ask students what Camila, Jaharlyn, and José Luis all have in common. (**van a la playa**)
- Ask whether the interviewees spend their vacations with family, friends, or both.
- The first **Panorama cultural** activity on Activity Master 3 is based on the first three interviews only.

Post-viewing
- Point out to students in an atlas where **Piñamar, Uruguay,** and **Puerto Cabello, Venezuela,** are located.
- Point out on an atlas where **Mar del Plata, Argentina; Punta del Este**, Uruguay; **San Carlos, Costa Rica;** and **Soria, España,** are located.
- Ask students which of the locations mentioned by the interviewees they would most like to visit and why.

Videoclips

- Ask students if they have ever heard of or visited a water park. Discuss different ways to have fun at a water park.
- Show the videoclip without sound and ask students to watch for the different kinds of slides, pools, and other ways of having fun at a water park. Ask students if they think water parks in Spain differ from those in the United States. If so, how?
- Play the videoclip with sound and ask students to write the year when the first water park was constructed in Spain. (1984)
- Ask students why there are so many water parks in Spain. (Warm climate and beaches bring millions of tourists to Spain.)

Colorín colorado

Have students write a journal entry about a real or imaginary vacation. They should write about where they went, what they did, and where they would like to go next time. You might want to play *Unas vacaciones ideales* again and use Ben's journal entry as a model.

Nombre _____ Clase _____ Fecha _____

Activity Master 1

De antemano *Unas vacaciones ideales*

<table>
<tr><td colspan="3">Supplementary Vocabulary</td></tr>
<tr><td>afuera outside</td><td>¡Es tremendo! It's great!</td><td>navegar to sail</td></tr>
<tr><td>la arena sand</td><td>las gafas de sol sunglasses</td><td>el/la vecino,-a neighbor</td></tr>
<tr><td>el barco de vela sailing ship</td><td>la isla island</td><td></td></tr>
</table>

Viewing

1. Which picture best illustrates Ben's idea of a fantasy vacation, and which one illustrates Carmen's idea? Write **Ben** or **Carmen** under each picture.

a. _____   b. _____

2. Write **C** for **cierto** or **F** for **falso** for each of the following statements.

_____ 1. Ben y Carmen no salen porque hace bastante mal tiempo hoy.

_____ 2. A Carmen le gustaría explorar el río Amazonas en canoa.

_____ 3. Ben y Carmen están aburridos.

_____ 4. La señora Corredor tiene una sorpresa para los muchachos.

Post-viewing

3. Fill in the crossword puzzle with the words that complete the following sentences. Then unscramble the five letters in the shaded boxes to find out where Ben and Carmen are going on their surprise trip.

1. _____ está escribiendo en su diario.
2. Ben quiere _____ todo el río Amazonas.
3. La señora Corredor se pone bloqueador porque hace sol en la _____.
4. La familia Corredor está en _____, Puerto Rico. (dos palabras)
5. La señora Corredor está leyendo una _____.
6. Ben y Carmen no quieren visitar a los _____.

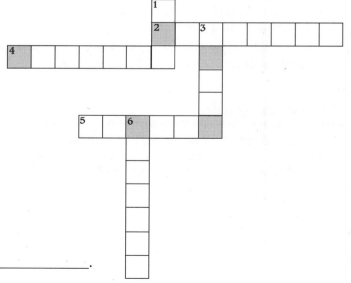

Ben y Carmen van a una _____.

Spanish 1 ¡Ven conmigo!

CAPÍTULO 12

Activity Master 2

Unas vacaciones ideales (a continuación)

Pre-viewing

1. Write two things you would expect to see in a tropical jungle.

    1. _____

    2. _____

Supplementary Vocabulary	
la catarata *waterfall*	la orquídea *orchid*
el diario *diary*	la pulgada *inch*
el impermeable *raincoat*	la rana *frog*
en peligro de extinción *endangered*	la serpiente *snake*
medir *to measure*	el tesoro *treasure*

Viewing

2. Place a check mark next to the items that señora Corredor says that Ben and Carmen need for their trip.

_____ **1.** la cámara   _____ **4.** las mochilas   _____ **7.** unos zapatos

_____ **2.** una corbata   _____ **5.** unos impermeables   _____ **8.** una chaqueta

_____ **3.** una maleta   _____ **6.** unas sandalias

Post-viewing

3. Based on what you saw, write **C** for **cierto** or **F** for **falso** next to each statement.

_____ **1.** Ben y Carmen necesitan hacer maletas.

_____ **2.** El abuelo no va a ir con Ben y Carmen.

_____ **3.** El coquí es una boa que mide casi doce pies.

_____ **4.** El Yunque es una selva tropical.

_____ **5.** Después de ir a El Yunque, Ben y Carmen están aburridos.

4. Put the following pictures in the order in which they occurred in the video. Then, write a sentence describing each scene.

        a.   **b.**   **c.**

_____ **1.** _____

_____

_____ **2.** _____

_____

_____ **3.** _____

_____

CAPÍTULO 12

Activity Master 3

Panorama cultural

Supplementary Vocabulary

escalar montes *to climb mountains*   la hacienda *ranch*
los familiares *relatives*   el novio *boyfriend*

Viewing

1. Match each person with all the things he or she does on vacation by checking the appropriate box(es).

	Camilia	Jaharlyn	José Luis
ver televisión			
ir a Uruguay			
dormir mucho			
ir a la playa			

2. Write **P** for **playa** next to the names of the people that go to the beach while on vacation.

_____ 1. Camila   _____ 4. Jennifer   _____ 7. Magaly

_____ 2. Jaharlyn   _____ 5. Santiago   _____ 8. Jaime

_____ 3. José Luis   _____ 6. Luis Alfonso   _____ 9. Shermine

3. Match the name of the person with what he or she does while on vacation.

_____ 1. Jennifer   **a.** ir a Chile, Mar del Plata y Punta del Este

_____ 2. Santiago   **b.** escalar montes

_____ 3. Jaime   **c.** jugar al voleibol

_____ 4. Shermine   **d.** montar en bicicleta

Videoclips

Supplementary Vocabulary

las anillas *rings, hoops*   los parques acúaticos *water parks*
las cascadas *waterfalls*   los ríos rápidos *rapids*
divertirse *to have fun*   los toboganes *slides*
las escaleras colgantes *rope ladders*   los tubos deslizantes *tube slides*

Viewing

4. Number the following water park attractions in the order in which you hear them.

_____ piscinas con escaleras colgantes   _____ tubos deslizantes   _____ toboganes

_____ ríos rápidos con cascadas   _____ anillas

5. Fill in the spaces with the correct numbers.

Se calcula que en todo el mundo existen actualmente unos _____ parques

acuáticos y España cuenta con un _____% de ellos, visitando sus instalaciones

anualmente unas _____ millones de personas.

Spanish 1 ¡Ven conmigo!

CAPÍTULO 12

Video Scripts

Video Program

CAPÍTULO PRELIMINAR
¡Adelante!

—¡Bienvenidos a Costa Rica!
—¡Bienvenidos a Venezuela!
—¡Bienvenidos a Argentina!
¡Bienvenido al mundo hispanohablante! Welcome to the Spanish-speaking world! Did you know that Spanish is spoken by over 300 million people in the world? It is spoken in Spain—where it originated—in Puerto Rico, and in 18 Latin American countries. In the Caribbean Islands of Cuba and the Dominican Republic; in Mexico and the Central American countries of Guatemala, Honduras, Nicaragua, El Salvador, Costa Rica, and Panama; and in South America, in the countries of Venezuela, Colombia, Ecuador, Peru, Bolivia, Chile, Argentina, Uruguay, and Paraguay. Spanish is spoken in parts of Africa and in the Philippines. It is also spoken by over 25 million people in the United States.

One of the first things you may want to do when learning a new language is to introduce yourself. Listen as these Spanish-speaking people tell you a little about themselves.
—Yo me llamo Jaime. Yo soy de Colombia. Yo tengo dieciséis años.
—Diego Varela y soy argentino pero nací en la Patagonia, Argentina, en la provincia del sur.
—Me llamo Ilda de Betencourt, Martínez de Betencourt. Soy de Caracas.
—Me llamo Jennifer y soy de Buenos Aires, Argentina.
—Yo me llamo Johnny José Martínez. Soy caraqueño, pertenezco a Venezuela.
—Yo me llamo Ana. Vivo en Madrid y tengo quince años.
—Me llamo Yamilé Anthony y soy de aquí, de Venezuela, Caracas.

If you're not sure you understand what someone says, you can always ask them to spell things out for you. Listen as Carla and Ellen say the Spanish alphabet.
—A, be, ce, che, de, e, efe, ge, ache, i, jota, ka, ele, elle, eme, [ene], eñe, o, pe, qu, ere, ese, te, u, uve, doble uve, equis, ye y zeta.

How many times a day do you use numbers? Giving someone your phone number, checking grades, and getting change at the store all involve numbers. Listen as Robi counts from one to eleven.
—Uno, dos, tres, cuatro, cinco, seis, siete, ocho, nueve, diez, once.

You're already well on your way to learning how to understand and communicate with Spanish speakers around the world!
—¡Hola! ¡Ven conmigo!

LOCATION OPENER:
España

—Hola, me llamo Paco. Soy de España, de Madrid. Ésta es la Plaza Mayor. Es bonita, ¿no? ¿Quieres ver más? Pues, ¡ven conmigo!

España... uno de los destinos turísticos más populares del mundo. Turistas vienen por las montañas nevadas, las playas blancas, las exquisitas comidas y por las ricas tradiciones culturales.

España es un país de muchas costas... ideal para la tabla vela y demás deportes acuáticos.

En el norte se puede esquiar en los Pirineos, las montañas que separan España del resto de Europa.

En marzo, Valencia se llena de gente para ver las fallas, figuras de cartón que serán quemadas.

En julio, durante las fiestas de los Sanfermines, los toros corren por las calles del centro de Pamplona.

Al centro del país... Madrid, capital de España. Una ciudad de museos, palacios, tiendas... ¡ciudad dinámica con una marcha increíble!

La arquitectura inimitable de Gaudí distingue a Barcelona, un centro industrial de España.

Sevilla, con toda su elegancia, es una de las ciudades más preciosas de Andalucía, en el sur de España.

Flores, molinos de viento, castillos medievales, ciudades cosmopolitas, pueblos tranquilos... Los distintos paisajes de España expresan la gran diversidad de su carácter.

CAPÍTULO 1
¡Mucho gusto!

De antemano
¡Me llamo Francisco!

—¡Ramón! ¡Hola! ¡Ramón!

—Hola, buenos días.

—Buenos días. ¿Cómo estás?

—Muy bien, gracias. ¿Y tú?

—¡Ay, Paco!

—Lo siento, mamá.

—Anda, vete.

—Gracias, mamá.

—¡Ramón!

—Hola, buenos días, Paco. ¿Cómo estás?

—Muy bien, gracias. ¿Hay una carta para mí?

—Paco, Paco, Paco, no. Ésta no es.

—Ésta es para el Sr. Francisco Xavier López Medina. Tú no te llamas Francisco. Tú te llamas Paco.

—Sí, ¡soy yo! ¡Soy yo! Yo soy Francisco, pero me llaman Paco.

—¡Gracias! Hasta luego, ¿eh?

—Adiós, don Francisco Xavier López Medina.

—Perdón, abuela.

—Hola, Francisco. Me llamo Mercedes Margarita Álvarez García y soy de Madrid. Tengo 15 años, me gusta la pizza y me gusta mucho el voleibol. ¿Cuántos años tienes? ¿Qué te gusta a ti? Hasta luego, Mercedes.

—¡Sí, señor! ¡Una carta de Mercedes! ¡Una chica fantástica!

—Me llamo Mercedes y soy de Madrid. Tengo 15 años. Me gusta la pizza y me gusta mucho el voleibol...

—Eres fantástica... Eres fenomenal.

—¡Paco! ¡Paco! Oye, está aquí tu amigo Felipe.

—Hola, Paco, ¿qué tal?

—Pues... excelente, gracias. ¿Y tú?

—¡Bien! Oye, ¿qué es eso?

—Es una carta.

—¿Una carta? ¿De quién?

—Pues... de una chica.

—¿Una chica? ¿Quién? ¿Cómo se llama?

—Felipe, es un secreto.

—Paco, soy tu amigo. Por favor... cuéntame.

—Bueno, mira...

¡Me llamo Francisco!
(a continuación)

—Oye, ¡qué formal! Sr. Francisco Xavier López Medina. ¿Eres tú, Paco?

—Sí... Se llama Mercedes... Es una chica fenomenal... ¡Es fantástica!

—¡Paco! Un momento, por favor.

—Eres mi amigo, ¿no? Necesito un favor. ¿Me ayudas?

—¿Qué? ¿Cómo?

—Escribe, por favor... Estoy muy nervioso. Querida Mercedes...

—Querida... Mercedes...

—Hola, ¿qué tal?

—Hola... ¿qué tal?

—Gracias por tu carta.

—Gracias por tu carta.

—Soy sincero, inteligente, organizado, alto y muy guapo. Sí, señor. Soy sincero... inteligente... organizado, alto y muy guapo.

—Soy sincero... inteligente... organizado, alto y muy guapo. ¡Guapísimo!

—Soy de Madrid...

—Soy... de Madrid...

—Tengo 15 años.

—Tengo 5 años...

—No, Felipe. Tengo 15 años.

—Bueno, ¿qué te gusta?

—Pues... Me gusta el fútbol... la biología... ¡ah!... ¡y me gusta mucho la pizza también! Mercedes, ¿conoces la pizzería Napoli? ¿Qué tal si tú y yo comemos una pizza el sábado en la pizzería Napoli? ¿A las cuatro, tal vez? Te espero allí. Hasta el sábado. Sinceramente, Francisco.

—¿Hay más?

—No, gracias. Eres un buen amigo.

—¿Paco?

—¿Merche?

—Pues... ¿Qué tal?

—Eh... muy bien. ¿Y tú?

—Pues, más o menos.

—Eh... Merche... éste es Felipe, mi amigo. Felipe, ésta es Merche, una chica de mi escuela.

—Mucho gusto, Merche.

—Igualmente.

—Felipe, Paco, ésta es mi amiga Juanita.

—Hola. ¿Qué tal?

—Bien, gracias.

—Hola.

—¿Qué haces aquí?

—Tengo una cita... a las cuatro...

—Yo también.

—Un momento, por favor.

—¡Ay, no! ¿Es posible? ¿Es él? Francisco... ¿Paco?... ¡Francisco! ¡Ay, no!

—¡Ay, no! ¿Es posible? ¿Es ella? Mercedes... ¿Merche?... ¡Mercedes! ¡Ay, no!

—¿Mercedes?

—¿Francisco?

—Vamos afuera.

—Juanita... éste es Francisco Xavier López Medina.

—Felipe... ésta es Mercedes Margarita Álvarez García.

—Pues, te gusta la pizza, ¿no?

—Sí.

Panorama cultural

Panorama cultural will introduce you to real Spanish speakers from around the globe, including Europe, Latin America, and the United States. In this chapter, we asked some people to tell us who they are and where they're from.

¿De dónde eres?

[Ivette] Mi nombre es Ivette Marcano. Soy de Ponce, Puerto Rico.

[Miguel] Hola, buenas tardes. Me llamo Miguel Silva. Tengo dieciséis años y soy de Madrid.

[Sandra] Yo me llamo Sandra Terán y soy de Venezuela.

[Mauricio] Me llamo Mauricio. Vivo aquí también en San José, Costa Rica y tengo quince años.

[Alfredo] Mi nombre es Alfredo Santiago Oliva Vinza y yo soy peruano.

[Gabriela] Me llamo Gabriela, eh... tengo diecisiete años y soy de acá de Argentina.

[Manolo] Me llamo Manolo Ábrego, tengo dieciséis años y soy de aquí de San Antonio.

[Alexis] Yo me llamo Alexis Severiche y ¿cuántos años tengo? Tengo dieciséis años y soy de Colombia, de Barrancabermeja.

[Laura] Me llamo Laura, tengo dieciséis años y soy de Sevilla.

[Jacó] Yo me llamo Jacó, tengo también..., no. Tengo diecisiete años y soy de Sevilla, también.

[Éric] Me llamo Éric Santiago. Soy de Puerto Rico.

[Henry] Mi nombre es Henry Cedillo, tengo quince años y soy de El Salvador.

[María Luisa] Me llamo María Luisa López. Yo soy de Quito, Ecuador y tengo quince años.

[Juan Carlos] Soy Juan Carlos Novoa y soy de aquí de Caracas de Venezuela.

[Aurora] Me llamo Aurora Montaño, soy de San Diego y tengo dieciséis.

[Teniente Pablo] Mi nombre es el teniente Pablo Daniel Ochoa y pertenezco al Regimiento Ganaderos a Caballo General San Martín.

[Janet] Mi nombre es Janet Molina y soy de Miami.

[Eduardo] Me llamo Eduardo Gurrola. Soy del Distrito Federal.

[Raquel] Mi nombre es Raquel Bravo y soy de Nicaragua. Managua, Nicaragua.

Videoclips

Colombia, tierra querida
himno de fe y armonía
cantemos, cantemos todos
grito de paz y alegría.
Vivemos, siempre vivemos a nuestra patria querida.
Su suelo es una oración
y es un canto de la vida.
Su suelo es una oración
y es un canto de la vida.
Cantando, cantando yo viviré.
Colombia, tierra querida.
Cantando, cantando yo viviré.
Colombia, tierra querida.
Colombia te hiciste grande
con el furor de tu gloria.
La América toda canta la floración de tu historia.
Vivemos, siempre vivemos
a nuestra patria querida.
Su suelo es una oración
y es un canto de la vida.
Su suelo es una oración
y es un canto de la vida.
Cantando, cantando yo viviré
Colombia, tierra querida.
Cantando, cantando yo viviré
Colombia, tierra querida.

CAPÍTULO 2
¡Organízate!

De antemano
¡Mañana es el primer día de clases!

—"De España vengo, de España soy. Y mi cuerpo serrano lo va diciendo. Y mi cuerpo serrano..."

—¡Abuela... Abuela... Abuela...!

—¡Ah! Paco. Buenas tardes, ¿cómo estás?

—Muy bien, abuela. ¿Y tú? De maravilla, ¿no?

—¡Sí, excelente! ¡Y tengo un nuevo disco compacto de zarzuela!

—Ah, ¿sí? Te gusta, ¿no?

—¡Ay! Me gusta mucho. Es fantástico.

—Abuela...

—Ay, lo siento, Paco. ¿Qué necesitas?

—Pues, abuela... Mañana es el primer día de clases y necesito muchas cosas.

—Ah, ¿sí? Dime, Paco, ¿qué cosas necesitas?

—Necesito una mochila, unos cuadernos, unos lápices, libros, papel, bolígrafos, una calculadora, un diccionario, unas zapatillas de tenis, eh... pósters, necesito pósters... Y un estéreo... No tengo un estéreo...

—Sí, sí. Ven conmigo, Paco... Ven conmigo. Paco, mira. ¡Tu cuarto es un desastre! Primero, organiza tu cuarto. Y ¿ves? Ya tienes lápices y toma, aquí tienes el dinero.

—Gracias, abuelita.

—Pero para las cosas que necesitas.

—Pero, abuelita, ¿organizar mi cuarto?

—¡Ay! Pobrecito...

—¿Ya estás listo?

—Sí, abuela, estoy listo.

—Bueno vamos a ver.

—Bueno, no necesito lápices, ni necesito bolígrafos.

—Sí, sí, tienes muchos, ¡pero yo no!

—Y ya tengo una calculadora.

—Bien.

—Pero no tengo mucho papel... y necesito más cuadernos. Y necesito también unas zapatillas de tenis. Y necesito una mochila... ¿Y un estéreo?

—Bueno, Paco. Ya tienes el dinero. Compra lo que necesitas, ¡pero sólo lo que necesitas!

—¿El dinero? ¿El dinero? ¿Dónde está el dinero?

¡Mañana es el primer día de clases!
(a continuación)

—¿El dinero? ¿El dinero? ¿Dónde está el dinero?

—¡Ay, por Dios! ¿Qué es esto?

—Lo siento, abuela... No sé dónde está el dinero.

—Eres un desastre, Paco. Venga, vamos a buscarlo. ¿No estará en tu escritorio? ¿Está en tu escritorio?

—No, aquí no está.

—Un zapato, la camiseta aquí. ¿Está debajo de la cama? ¡Vaya por Dios! Un diccionario, ropa, libros, papeles, un reloj. Mira Paco, ya tienes una mochila... y el dinero.

—Muchas gracias, abuela. ¡Eres fenomenal!

—Bueno, bueno, ahora vete.

—Gracias, abuela. Hasta luego.

—Paco es un poco desorganizado, pero es mi nieto favorito. Y bueno, sólo tengo un nieto.

—Siete... uno... seis... cuatro... nueve... tres.

—¿Diga?

—Hola, habla Paco.

—¿Qué tal, hombre?

—Pues, regular. Necesito comprar unas cosas para mañana. ¿Me quieres acompañar?

—Sí, perfecto. ¿Dónde y a qué hora?

—En la plaza de Santa Ana, en veinte minutos.

—Vale, hasta luego.

—Hasta luego.

—Buenas tardes. ¿Qué queréis?

—Necesito papel.

—¿Cuántos paquetes?

—Eh... dos, por favor. Eh... no, tres, por favor.

—Tres. ¿Algo más?

—Sí, unas gomas, por favor.

—¿Cuántas?

—Eh... cuatro. ¡No, cinco! Sí, sí. Cinco, por favor.

—¿Seguro?

—Sí, cinco, por favor.

—¿Qué más?

—Necesito cinco cuadernos, por favor. No, no. Necesito uno azul, dos rojos, uno amarillo y uno verde.

—Bueno, uno azul, dos rojos, uno amarillo y uno verde. ¿Qué más?

—No, nada. Sí, perfecto.

—Muchas gracias.

—De nada, gracias a ti.

—Hola, buenas tardes. ¿Qué queréis?

—Pues, necesito unas zapatillas de tenis como éstas.

—Muy bien, y ¿qué número tienes?

—Treinta y nueve.

—Perfecto.

—Aquí tienes tus zapatillas.

—Gracias.

—Mmm, no, no me gustan. No, este estilo no me gusta.

—Pues no hay más estilos. ¿Vais a comprar algo?

—Lo siento mucho, señor, pero hoy no. Felipe, tengo otra idea.

—¿Qué es?

—Ven conmigo.

—Lo siento de verdad.

—Más lo siento yo.

Capítulo 2 *cont.*
Panorama cultural

In this chapter, we asked some people what they need to buy before the school year starts.

¿Qué necesitas para el colegio?

[Paulina] Tengo que comprar todos los cuadernos, los libros y mi uniforme.

[Jimena] Tuve que comprar lápices, lapiceras, gomas, eh... reglas, cartuchera, mochila, cuadernos y carpetas.

[Fabiola] Bueno, cuadernos, lápices, libros, borradores, eh... calculadora, cuadernos, libros, borrador, lápiz, diccionario.

[Tomás] Bueno, en año escolar no se necesita comprar libros, no más llevar papel, lápiz, pluma, cuaderno y estar preparado con lo que te van a dar.

[Brenda] Los libros que me piden, cuadernos, plumas, este... libros, la mochila, eh... cuadernos, ¿qué más? este... plumas y el uniforme.

[Johnny] ¿Qué necesito comprar? Libros, cuadernos, libretas, bloc, este... una gran cantidad de lápices, etcétera.

[Miguel] Pues material escolar, goma, bolígrafo, lapiceros, etcétera.

[Caroline] Cuando comienza el año escolar, tenemos que comprar polos blancas, faldas, medias, zapatos, las libretas, los libros, el bulto. El bulto, en el bulto tengo los bolígrafos, los lápices, la libreta, un diccionario y mi cartera.

[Julieta] No sé, biromes, carpetas, hojas —¿eso me preguntas? Sí, los libros para estudiar.

[Ángel] Libros, cuadernos, lápices... La calculadora, lápiz y borrador.

[Carlos] Cuadernos, este... libros, este... puede ser plumas, lápices, este... pegamentos, una flauta para música, una lapicera.

Videoclips

Ya sabes por qué tú has llegado más lejos que él. Léete un libro.

—Hola, yo me llamo María Inés y soy de México, de la ciudad de Cuernavaca. Ésta es la Plaza de Armas. ¿Te gusta? ¿Quieres ver más? Pues, ¡ven conmigo!

México... un país rico... por su historia, su cultura y también por sus recursos naturales.

La capital de México es la ciudad más grande del mundo, con más de veinte millones de habitantes...

Acero, automóviles, energía eléctrica... todos hechos en México...

El pintoresco pueblo de Taxco es la capital de la platería, una artesanía conocida mundialmente.

Mucho antes de la llegada de los españoles, varias civilizaciones indígenas construyeron grandes ciudades, con una arquitectura que todavía sorprende por su belleza y esplendor.

Las distintas culturas de México han formado un caleidoscopio de sones, ritmos, sabores y colores.

CAPÍTULO 3
Nuevas clases, nuevos amigos

De antemano
¡Bienvenida al colegio!

—Bueno, ya son las ocho menos cinco, ¿lista? ¿Qué te pasa, Claudia? ¿Estás nerviosa?
—Sí, un poco.
—Está bien, los alumnos de este colegio son muy amables.
—¿Y qué clase tengo ahora?
—Ah... el horario. Aquí tienes el horario de clase. Ahorita tienes clase de ciencias sociales. A las ocho cincuenta tienes clase de francés. El descanso es a las nueve cuarenta. Después tienes a las diez química, computación, geometría, educación física y español. ¿Bien?
—Gracias.
—Atención, muchachos, por favor. Buenos días.
—Buenos días.
—Ella es una compañera nueva. Se llama Claudia Obregón Sánchez y es de la ciudad de México. Siéntense, por favor.
—Hola, ¿qué tal, Claudia? Me llamo María Inés Hernández.
—Hola.

—Y yo soy Fernando Rodríguez. Encantado y
¡bienvenida a Cuernavaca!

—Mucho gusto, Fernando, y gracias.

—¿Eres de la ciudad de México?

—Sí, sí.

—¡Ay, qué padre! A mí me gusta mucho la capital.
Hay muchas cosas interesantes allá, ¿no?

—Sí, sí, la capital es muy divertida.

—Profesor... Buenos días, profesor Romanca.

—Buenos días, señor Altamirano.

—¿Está aquí la nueva estudiante?

—Sí, está en la clase. Se llama Claudia Obregón
Sánchez.

—Claudia... Obregón... Sánchez... Sánchez.

—Gracias, Señor Director.

—Hasta luego, profesor.

—Mira... me gusta ir al parque con mi familia y
también me gusta visitar los museos. Son
buenos. Éste es el Museo Antropológico y ella es
una amiga. A ella le gusta ir a los museos también.

—A mí no me gustan los museos. Son aburridos.
¡Pero me gusta ir a los parques!

—Oye, ella es muy bonita, ¿eh?

—Y también es muy buena onda. Mira, mira esta
foto. También me gusta mucho jugar al básquetbol.

—A mi amigo Luis le gusta mucho jugar al básquetbol también. Miren, ya son las ocho. ¿Y
dónde está el profesor?

—Fernando, ¿cómo es esta clase? ¿Te gusta?

—¡Ay no! Esta clase es horrible. El profesor es
muy aburrido, hay mucha tarea todos los días y
muchos exámenes... Híjole, los exámenes son
muy difíciles y al profesor no le gustan los
exámenes fáciles.

—¡No hombre!

—No te preocupes, Claudia, no es verdad. Esta
clase es mi favorita. Y es muy interesante, y el
profesor, pues es... así... Ejém, buenos días,
clase. Clase, ¡buenos días!

—Buenos días.

—Sr. Rodríguez, una pregunta. ¿Le gustan las
ciencias sociales?

—Pues, sí, profesora, me gustan.

—¿Y le gusta estudiar?

—Sí, profesora, me gusta estudiar.

—Entonces, Rodríguez... ¿Por qué no le gusta estudiar ciencias sociales? Bueno, clase, abran sus
libros en la página 26.

¡Bienvenida al colegio!
(a continuación)

—Como saben, México es una república federal.
Sr. Rodríguez, por favor, ¿cuánto tiempo está el
presidente a cargo?

—Por seis años, profesor.

—Bien, Sr. Rodríguez. Ya casi son las ocho cincuenta. Ésta es la tarea para mañana.

—Adiós, clase. Señorita Hernández, un momento
por favor en el patio.

—Sí, profesor.

—Generalmente, eres una alumna responsable y
seria... una buena alumna. Pero hoy no, ¿por
qué?

—No sé. De verdad, no sé. Lo siento, profesor.

—A ver... A causa de tus acciones esta mañana en
clase, tengo un trabajo especial para ti. Te gusta
hablar frente a la clase, ¿verdad? Pues aquí
tienes un artículo. Para mañana necesitas leer el
artículo y preparar una presentación para la
clase.

—Está bien, profesor.

—Oye, ¿qué pasó con el profesor?

—Ay, ahora tengo una tarea adicional y larga.

—Híjole, qué mala onda.

—Bueno, no hay problema... Uy, qué día y sólo
son las ocho cincuenta de la mañana... Ay, por
fin son las dos y media. Oye, Claudia, vamos al
patio y te presento a unos amigos.

—Sí, vamos.

—¡Hola! Les presento a una compañera nueva.
Se llama Claudia Obregón y es de la capital.

—Oye, ¿quién es ese chico alto con Fernando?

—Se llama Luis. ¡Es muy simpático! Vamos.

—¡Hola, chicas!

—¡Hola! Ella es Claudia Obregón. Claudia, te presento a Luis Barajas. Claudia es de la capital.

—Hola, mucho gusto.

—Mucho gusto.

—Hola.

—Y tú, ¿qué tal?

—Bueno, más o menos. Tengo una tarea muy
larga para mañana.

—Para el profesor de ciencias sociales, ¿verdad?

—Fernando... Sí, desgraciadamente.

—Oigan, ¿vamos por unas paletas?

—Bueno, sí.

—¡Ay!, yo no puedo. Ya tengo planes. Necesito ir
al trabajo a las tres de la tarde y ya son veinte
para las tres. Vamos.

—Luis, Claudia dice que le gusta mucho el básquetbol. Tienen algo en común. A Luis le gusta
mucho también. Es muy bueno para el básquet.

—¿Sí? ¡Qué padre!

—¿Juegas mucho al básquet?

—Sí. En mi colegio en la capital, jugaba todos los
días.

—Y el colegio en la Ciudad de México, ¿cómo es?
¿Grande?

—Sí, es grande. En las clases hay más estudiantes
que aquí. Muchas veces hay cincuenta estudiantes en una sola clase.

—¡Híjole! ¡Qué difícil! ¡Cincuenta estudiantes!

—Pues, allá es normal.

—¿Y las clases? ¿Son más fáciles?

—No sé... no creo. Allá, los profesores dan mucha
tarea también y son bastante estrictos.

Capítulo 3 *cont.*

—Pues, con cincuenta estudiantes, ser estricto es necesario, ¿no?

—Sí, es necesario... sobre todo con los estudiantes más cómicos... o cómicas, depende...

—También con las estudiantes que son buenas actrices.

—Sí, también con las buenas actrices...

—Uy, por favor, qué malos son.

Panorama cultural

In this chapter, we asked some students at what time they usually go to school, what they do after class and which classes they like.

¿Cómo es un día escolar típico?

[Mario] Bueno... son varios horarios. En el horario de la mañana voy a las siete de la mañana, y en el horario de la tarde a las doce y media, más o menos.

[Natalie] Eh... ¿un día normal? Bueno... voy a la escuela de siete de la mañana a una y media de la tarde. De ahí voy a mi casa, almuerzo. Normalmente después me acuesto como hasta las tres de la tarde y después me pongo a estudiar si tengo algo que estudiar.

[Lucía] Bueno... el día es tranquilo. En general es lindo. Me la paso bien acá dentro del colegio y tengo alrededor de doce materias. Mi materia preferida es literatura y todas las que tengan que ver con lo humanístico.

[Omar] Me levanto a la mañana, voy al colegio, si tengo tarea hago los deberes, y después salgo, vengo a la plaza, salgo.

[Erika] Pues me levanto, me baño, me voy a la escuela, estudiamos, nos salimos a descanso, regresamos, seguimos estudiando y nos dan salida.

[Ángela] Sí, este... son doce lecciones diarias entre ésa y dos recreos grandes y una hora de almuerzo.

[Gala] Bueno, entro al colegio a las ocho de la mañana y me quedo allí hasta las doce y media que salgo para almorzar. Después entro a las dos menos diez, menos viente, por ahí, y salgo a las cuatro y media.

[Juan] Pues se empieza el día desde las ocho de la mañana. Este, hay dos materias, un descanso, dos materias tres horas después y salida.

[Vivian] Tengo siete clases al día. Son inglés, matemáticas, química, ah... gimnasia, español y literatura española. Y mi más favorita tiene que ser matemáticas.

[Juan Carlos] Bueno... normal, o sea llegamos, entramos a los salones, vemos clases, tenemos nuestro recreo. Después al mediodía nos vamos para la casa a comer y en la tarde volvemos al colegio.

[Lucila] A la mañana entramos a las ocho y cuarto y nos vamos a comer cada uno a su casa o adonde quiera ir a comerse a las doce y cuarto. Y durante la hora del colegio tenemos matemáticas, lengua... Hoy por ejemplo tenemos taller, computación, inglés.

Videoclips

A veces no disfrutamos de la Navidad y del Año Nuevo por estar llamando al exterior. Pero, deténgase. Desde el 20 de diciembre de las diez de la noche hasta las siete de la mañana del 2 de enero todos tendrán tiempo de hacer sus llamadas a cualquier hora del día con las tarifas super-reducidas de Mida. Ahora, sí, disfrute de sus fiestas. No espere que den las doce del 24 o del 31 de diciembre y rompa las barreras del cariño.

—¿Aló? Ja, ja, ja. Yo también te deseo una feliz Navidad.

CAPÍTULO 4
¿Qué haces esta tarde?

De antemano
¿Dónde está María Inés?

—¿Quién?

—Soy Luis.

—Sí, un momento.

—Sí, gracias.

—Hola.

—Hola. ¿Cómo estás, Luis?

—Bien, Claudia, ¿y tú?

—De maravilla. Ven, te presento a mi familia. Hola, papi. Él es mi amigo Luis.

—Hola.

—Luis, él es mi padre.

—Ah... sí... sí... Luis, ¡mucho gusto!

—Igualmente, Sr. Obregón.

—Después de la clase yo canto en el coro con Luis.

—Sí, yo sé. Los miércoles y los viernes, ¿verdad?

—No, papi, los martes y los jueves.

—Entonces, Luis, ¿vas a Taxco con Claudia y Rosa?

—Sí, señor, voy con ellas.

—¿Y dónde está Rosa?

—Está en la sala. Bueno, jóvenes, hasta luego... Voy al mercado. ¿Necesitas algo Claudia?

—No, gracias. Ven, Rosa está en la sala.

—Hola, Rosa. Él es mi amigo Luis.

—Hola, Luis. Claudia habla mucho de ti. Hmm... tú juegas al básquetbol muy bien, ¿no?... ah... y tocas la guitarra también. Tienes mucho talento, ¿verdad?

—Pues... no sé.

—Bueno, Luis, vamos a Taxco porque mañana es el cumpleaños de mamá, y mi tío Ernesto tiene un regalo especial para ella. Como muchas personas en Taxco, mi tío Ernesto trabaja con la plata. Es un platero excelente.

—¿Va también Julio? Julio es mi hermano y tiene dieciocho años.

—No, no va. Anita llega a las tres de la tarde.

—Ah... es cierto. Mira, él es Julio y ella es Anita. Anita es su novia y son inseparables. Ella es de Puebla. Cuando Anita está aquí en Cuernavaca, Julio pasa todo el día con ella. A veces pasean en bicicleta y a veces van a la alberca. ¿Qué hacen hoy?

—Hoy van al cine.

—Ah... ¡Tengo una muy buena idea! A María Inés le gusta mucho Taxco. Tal vez pueda ir con nosotros. ¿Está bien, Rosa? ¿Llamo a María Inés?

—Sí, cómo no, buena idea.

—Ah, pero los sábados por la mañana, María Inés practica con su grupo de baile folklórico.

—Pues, vamos allá. La escuela de baile donde tiene clase está en la avenida Juárez.

—Muy bien. Rosa, ¿a qué hora vamos a Taxco?

—A la una.

—Está bien. Hasta luego.

—Chao.

—Adiós.

—Chao, María Inés.

—Hasta luego.

—Oye, voy al centro. ¿Me acompañas?

—Gracias, Juan, pero no puedo. Necesito ir al correo. Adiós.

—Adiós.

—Disculpa, ¿está aquí María Inés Hernández?

—No, va ahorita hacia el correo.

—¿Al correo? ¿Vamos allá?

—Sí vamos, pero... ¿Dónde está?

—En la plaza de la Constitución.

—Bueno, gracias.

—Adiós.

—Adiós.

—Bueno, ¿qué hacemos? ¿Regresamos a casa?

—Sí, aquí no está.

—Vamos. Momento... por lo general estudia en la biblioteca después de bailar. ¿Por qué no vamos allá?

—Sí, ¿por qué no?

—Vamos. Qué pena. María Inés no está en la escuela de baile, no está en el correo y no está aquí en la biblioteca. ¿Qué hacemos?

—Bueno, no sé. Vamos a Taxco a la una, ¿no?

—Sí y son las doce y media. No hay remedio. Vamos a casa.

¿Dónde está María Inés? *(a continuación)*

—Qué pena. María Inés no está en la escuela de baile, no está en el correo y no está aquí en la biblioteca. ¿Qué hacemos?

—Bueno, no sé. Vamos a Taxco a la una, ¿no?

—Sí y son las doce y media. No hay remedio. Vamos a casa.

—Buenos días, Sr. Obregón. ¿Cómo está?

—Muy bien, gracias. ¿Y tú, María Inés?

—Bien, también, gracias. ¿Está aquí, Claudia?

—No, no está.

—Bueno, gracias. Hasta luego.

—Mira, es ella.

—¡María Inés! ¡María Inés!

—¡Claudia! ¡Luis! ¡Qué suerte!

—Hola. Oye, María Inés, ¿qué haces aquí? Te buscamos por todas partes —en la escuela de baile, en el correo y en la biblioteca.

—Pues, estoy aquí porque tengo la tarde libre. ¿Ustedes qué hacen esta tarde?

—Ah, están aquí. ¿Listos? Hola, María Inés. ¿Qué pasa? ¿Vas con nosotros?

—¿Mande? ¿Adónde van?

—Vamos a Taxco. ¿Quieres ir también?

—¿A Taxco? Pues... sí, claro. Pero, por favor, primero llamo a mi mamá para pedirle permiso. ¿A qué hora regresamos?

—Regresamos a las ocho, más o menos.

—Bueno. ¿Puedo hablar por teléfono?

—Claro chica. Entra... está en la sala.

—Toma.

—¡Vamos! Mi mamá dice que está bien.

—¡Ay, qué bien! ¡Qué padre! ¡Vámonos!

—Tío Ernesto no está todavía aquí. Llegamos un poco temprano. Los sábados por la tarde tío Ernesto va al parque y juega al fútbol con sus amigos y no regresa sino hasta las cuatro. ¿Por qué no paseamos un poco por Taxco?

—¡Sí! Taxco es muy bonito.

—Y es la primera vez que yo estoy aquí.

—¿En serio? ¡Qué suerte! Hoy comienza la Feria de la Plata y hay un desfile de niños.

—¡Qué padre! Pues vamos.

—Vamos.

—Son cuatro y diez. Tío Ernesto debe estar ya en la tienda. ¿Vamos?

—¡Vamos!

—¡Están aquí! ¡Qué bien! ¡Bienvenidos!

—Gracias.

—Pero desafortunadamente, yo necesito estar aquí en la tienda hasta las seis y sólo son las cuatro y cuarto...

—Bueno... tengo una idea. María Inés, Luis y yo queremos ver más de Taxco. ¿Podemos ir al teleférico? ¿Está bien?

—Claro, Claudia. Es buena idea. Y después, vamos a mi casa, ¿sí?

Capítulo 4 cont.

—Sí, está bien. Pero yo no voy con ustedes. Me quedo aquí, con tío Ernesto.
—Bueno, hasta pronto.
—Adiós.
—Mira esta pieza, Rosa. Es bonita, ¿no?
—Sí, es preciosa.
—Es una de mis favoritas. Ven, te enseño más. Vamos al taller.
—Taxco es una ciudad muy hermosa.
—¿Por qué no sacas unas fotos aquí?
—Bueno. Buena idea.
—Claudia, ¿qué es eso?
—Ésa es la Iglesia de Santa Prisca.
—Son las cinco y media. ¿Regresamos a la tienda?
—Sí.
—Vamos.
—¿Y qué tal?
—¡Muy bien!
—Taxco me gusta muchísimo.
—Sí, el teleférico es muy divertido.
—Mira, Claudia... Éste es el regalo para tu mamá.
—¡Tío Ernesto! ¡Es una maravilla!
—Sí... ¡Es fantástica! A mamá le va a gustar mucho.
—Muchísimas gracias, tío Ernesto.
—Sí, gracias.
—Bueno, bueno, ya está bien. Ahora ¡vamos a casa! Allí tenemos otras sorpresas —¡enchiladas, refrescos y helado para todos!
—¡Qué rico!
—Yo quiero uno de arroz.
—Yo quiero uno de chocolate.

Panorama cultural

The paseo is a tradition in Spanish-speaking countries; people stroll around the plaza or along the streets of a town in the evening to socialize, and to see and be seen by others. In this chapter we asked some teenagers if they enjoy the **paseo** and what they do.

¿Te gusta pasear con tus amigos?

[Patricia] Me gusta ir con mis amigos a las tiendas, de compras.... Me gusta ir mucho, como le dije, al parque, para ir a ver a los muchachos y también a la playa.

[David] Sí, con mis amigos sí me gusta pasear... Podemos ir de la casa de uno o a la casa de otro.

[Juan Pablo] Sí, me gusta pasear. Vamos a la Cartuja, a María Luisa y hablamos de todo un poco. Que aquí en Sevilla es que es muy común, si no se sale de vacaciones, dar una vuelta ya que con el verano el calor la casa es un infierno... y vamos, se pasa bien aquí con los amigos.

[Jimena] Vamos a pasear. Vamos a muchísimos lugares... Y porque me parece divertido estar todos juntos. Es una manera de hacerse más amigos de todos.

[Jeimmy] Sí me gusta para... sí, me gusta hacer paseos, y me, y porque yo comparto con mis compañeros y paseamos juntos.

[Leslie] Me gusta pasear con ellos porque son divertidos y vamos a dar la vuelta por todo el pueblo.

[Claudia] A mí me encanta dar paseos, me gusta divertirme mucho con la familia y con las amigas. Nomás, me gusta divertirme.

[Kevin] Bueno, me gusta dar paseos con mis amigos. Vamos a la playa.

Videoclips

—Listos. Vamos a comenzar.
También con las manos se pueden mover los pies. Porque ningún hombre es menos válido que otro, apoya a Teletón. El Banco Popular ya lo está haciendo.

LOCATION OPENER: Florida

¡Hola! Me llamo Raquel Villanueva y soy de Miami. Miami es una ciudad muy interesante. ¿Te gustaría ver más? Bueno, ¡ven conmigo!

Por su agradable clima, sus hermosas playas, sus parques y su ambiente cosmopolita, la Florida es uno de los estados más visitados...

Uno de los lugares más alegres es Miami, una verdadera capital de América Latina...

Millones de latinoamericanos vienen para visitar a sus familiares, hacer compras o conocer los parques.

La mayoría de los hispanohablantes en la Florida son cubanos. Los cubanoamericanos han mantenido su idioma y sus costumbres...

En la Pequeña Habana hay tiendas, restaurantes y locales donde solamente se habla español. Pero Miami abarca grandes comunidades centroamericanas y sudamericanas también.

La Florida es hogar de muchas otras comunidades étnicas... un lugar donde hay mucho que ver y hacer... un estado fascinante.

CAPÍTULO 5
El ritmo de la vida

De antemano
¿Cómo es el ritmo de tu vida?

—¡Bienvenidos! Hoy es el seis de noviembre y ésta es la nueva edición de "Noticias Colegio Seminole". Yo soy Patricia Carter...

—Yo soy José Luis Jiménez. Como siempre, tenemos un programa muy interesante para ustedes esta semana. Pero primero... ¿qué tiempo hace? Aquí en Miami, hace buen tiempo. Hace mucho sol; en Nueva York hace un poco de frío... La temperatura allá está a 36 grados. ¡Uf! En Chicago está nevando. La ciudad ya tiene tres pulgadas de nieve. En California hace un poco de viento hoy... y en Texas, está lloviendo a cántaros.

—Gracias, José Luis. Ahora, vamos al reportaje especial de Raquel. Esta semana, ella habla con la gente del colegio sobre el ritmo de sus actividades en una semana típica.

—¡Hola a todos! Raquel Villanueva, a sus órdenes. Todos nosotros estamos aquí, en el colegio, durante las horas de clase. ¿Pero qué hacemos cuando no estamos aquí? Ramón, ¿qué haces tú por la tarde?

—Bueno, los martes y los jueves, trabajo en el restaurante de mi padre. Y cuando no trabajo, hago la tarea o paso el rato con mis amigos.

—Gracias, Ramón.

—¿Qué tal, Anita y Josué? Dime, Anita... ¿qué haces típicamente los domingos?

—Eh... todos los domingos, descanso y leo el periódico. Y Josué y yo siempre corremos juntos por la tarde.

—Ah, ¿sí? ¿Y corren mucho?

—Sí, mucho. Nos gusta correr. Pero en el verano no, porque hace demasiado calor.

—Buenos días, profesor Williams.

—Buenos días, Raquel.

—¿Qué hace usted por la noche cuando está en casa?

—Bueno, Raquel... primero la señora Williams y yo preparamos la cena, y después, a veces escucho música o escribo cartas.

—Tenemos un nuevo estudiante en el Colegio Seminole. ¿Quién es? Es Armando Tamayo y es de Panamá.

—¡Bienvenido al Colegio Seminole, Armando! Armando, ¿qué haces en tu tiempo libre?

—Bueno, en mi tiempo libre, yo pinto y dibujo.

—¿En serio? A mí también me gusta mucho pintar y dibujar. Qué casualidad, ¿no? Bueno, amigos. Aquí termina mi reportaje. Quiero recibir tarjetas postales de ustedes. ¿Les gusta el programa? ¡Escríbanme! Y hasta la próxima.

—Gracias, Raquel... y ahora...

—¡Ay no!

—¿Qué pasa? ¿Hay un problema con la cámara?

—¡Ernesto! Por favor, ven aquí. ¡Rápido!

¿Cómo es el ritmo de tu vida?
(a continuación)

—¡Ernesto! ¡El letrero del programa!

—Gracias por su atención, pero hoy tenemos algunos problemitas técnicos. Ustedes comprenden, ¿no? A seguir, muchachos.

—Gracias, Sra. Fajardo. Hace mucho calor hoy en el estudio, y... hace mucho calor aquí en Miami. Hace calor... Sí señor, hace calor.

—Eh... de acuerdo, Patricia. Hace calor en Miami hoy.

—Y hablando de calor, José Luis, nuestro club de ecología necesita voluntarios este sábado. Vamos a participar en un programa para limpiar una sección de la bahía Bizcayne. Van a participar muchas escuelas secundarias de Miami. La bahía es uno de los lugares más bonitos de aquí y es muy importante mantenerla limpia. Todo el grupo sale del colegio a las diez de la mañana el sábado.

—Y el club de ciencias tiene una reunión el sábado por la tarde —a las tres— en el planetario del Museo de las Ciencias y el Espacio. Vamos a ver un programa especial sobre el planeta Júpiter. Y el programa no es sólo para los estudiantes del club de ciencias. Todos los estudiantes del Colegio Seminole son invitados.

—Gracias por su atención, televidentes. Nos vemos.

—Hasta el próximo programa.

—¡Corte!

—¡Huy! ¡Qué desastre!

—No está tan mal. Estos problemitas ocurren algunas veces. Bien, guarden sus cosas, por favor, y un buen fin de semana para todos.

—Su programa es muy divertido, Raquel.

—Bueno, hoy más divertido que lo normal. Qué lío, ¿verdad?

—¿Qué vamos a hacer mañana? ¿Tienen planes?

—Bueno, como Armando no conoce Miami muy bien, ¿por qué no vamos al Museo Vizcaya?

—Ay, perfecto. Los jardines son maravillosos.

—De acuerdo. ¿Qué te parece Armando?

—Sí, vamos.

—A mí me encanta Vizcaya, las flores....

—¡Júpiter!

—¿Qué dices? ¿Qué qué?

—¡Júpiter! ¡El planeta Júpiter! ¡El programa sobre el planeta Júpiter en el planetario a las tres!

—¿Y qué hora es?

—¡Son las tres y cinco! ¡Tengo que ir!

—¿Por qué no... no vamos todos?

—Hace mucho calor aquí...

—Ay, sí, es verdad. Hace mucho calor...

—Y el planetario tiene aire acondicionado.

—Vamos al planetario.

Capítulo 5 cont.
Panorama cultural

In this chapter, we asked some students what they usually do during the week and on weekends.

¿Cómo es una semana típica?

[Matías] Vengo al colegio a las ocho y cuarto; salgo doce y cuarto para irme a comer; vuelvo a la una y media y salgo de nuevo a las cuatro y cuarto. Llego a mi casa, veo tele y como y voy a dormir.

[María Luisa] ¿Una semana normal? Vengo al colegio y del colegio a la casa, y... de ahí no hago nada más.

[Maikel] Ir al liceo, llegar a casa en la tarde, hacer mis tareas y descansar.

¿Y los fines de semana?

[Matías] Voy a andar en velero, al club náutico y después vuelvo tarde a eso de las ocho y vuelvo a mi casa directo a dormir.

[María Luisa] Salgo a comer con mis amigas, me voy a casa de ellas, o ellas vienen a mi casa.

[Maikel] Bueno quedarme en mi casa o sino salgo con mis padres.

[Lucía] Bueno, vengo al cole, y después del cole hago distintas cosas —qué sé yo— por ejemplo, juego al paddle, o a mí me gusta la música entonces estoy en mi casa y toco la guitarra, o a veces miro tele, pero muy poco. O leo también.

[Marcelo] Bueno, yo voy a la escuela a estudiar, de ahí regreso, juego, miro televisión, y los fines de semana yo voy a comer fuera y me divierto.

[Guido] Salgo del colegio, en mi casa como, después me voy a trabajar, llego a casa y hago la tarea —supuestamente— y nada más, miro televisión.

[Jesús] ¿Una semana típica? Bueno, estudiar desde el día lunes hasta el día viernes, tratar de hacer toda la tarea los días de, de los cinco días primeros de la semana y luego el fin de semana ir al Ávila o a disfrutar un poco.

[Juan Fernando] Bueno, de lunes a viernes, una semana corriente sería ir al colegio, hacer las tareas y descansar un poco.

¿Y los fines de semana?

[Lucía] Bueno, los fines de semana salgo con mi novio, con amigos, y vamos, vamos a... de todo un poco, a cualquier lado.

[Juan Fernando] Los sábados y domingos, eh... practico deportes.

[Guido] Fines de semana voy a bailar y no sé, un montón de cosas, no me acuerdo ahora.

Según el Instituto Meteorológico el siguiente es el pronóstico del tiempo para esta tarde. El Valle Central estará nublado con aislados aguaceros. La temperatura será de 28 grados. Guanacaste reportará lluviosidad parcial con aisladas lluvias. La temperatura llegará a los 31 grados. El sector pacífico del país, el cielo estará nublado con aislados aguaceros. La temperatura será de 31 grados. En la zona norte estará nublado con aguaceros. La vertiente del Caribe tendrá nubosidad parcial y aislados aguaceros sobre el sector montañoso. La temperatura llegará a los 30 grados.

CAPÍTULO 6
Entre familia

De antemano
¿Cómo es tu familia?

—Parece que mi madre todavía no está aquí. Hola, Pepe...
—Hola, lindo.
—Vamos... ¿Tomamos un jugo?
—Sí, perfecto.
—Pues, vamos a la cocina. Ven, Pepe... Ven, Pepe. El jugo está en el refrigerador.
—A ver, Raquel... ¿cómo es tu familia?
—Bueno, es bastante grande. Tengo tres hermanos, una hermana y muchísimos primos.
—¿Y cuántos viven aquí?
—Somos ocho en casa: mis padres, todos mis hermanos menos uno, una abuela y una tía. Gracias.
—¿Y cómo son tus padres? ¿Son simpáticos?
—Sí, son muy simpáticos. ¿Por qué no miramos mi álbum de fotos? Así puedes conocer a toda la familia.
—Pues, vamos.
—Éstos son mis padres. Ellos son de Cuba. Les gusta mucho trabajar en el jardín. Mi mamá es muy buena cocinera. Alguna vez debes probar la barbacoa que ella prepara. ¡Es fenomenal!
—¿Quiénes son ellos?
—Éstos son mis hermanos mayores. Y ella es mi hermana menor.
—¿Y esta chica que toca la flauta?

—Soy yo. No seas tonto.

—Ustedes son una familia muy unida, ¿verdad?

—Sí, nosotros hacemos muchas cosas juntos, especialmente los domingos. Mira esta foto... Primero, vamos a la iglesia. Después, comemos juntos y salimos a alguna parte. En esta foto, salimos al parque.

—¿Quién es esta señora alta y elegante?

—Es la hermana de mi mamá. Es divorciada y vive con nosotros. Y mira... aquí estamos en el parque. A mis hermanos les gusta mucho jugar al fútbol americano... y a mí también. Juego con ellos un poco todos los fines de semana y comemos, bebemos...

—¿Qué comen?

—Uy, comemos de todo... arroz con frijoles negros, maduros, tostones, pollo asado... Umm, el pollo asado de mi tía Gloria es fenomenal. Mira, aquí hay una foto de nuestro perro Pepe y de mí.

—Ay, qué lindo es. Y es cariñoso, ¿verdad?

—Sí, Pepe es muy cariñoso y....

—¿Qué es eso?

—Ay, no... ¿Dónde está Pepe?

¿Cómo es tu familia?
(a continuación)

—Ay, no, mira. Pepe, eres un desastre. Anda, vete. ¡Afuera! Ahora tengo que limpiar este lío, y es tu culpa. Por favor traeme la escoba... Gracias.

—De nada. Además de cariñoso, Pepe es un poco travieso, ¿verdad?

—No, no es un poco travieso... ¡Es muy travieso!

—¿Cuántos años tiene Pepe?

—A ver... ahora tiene casi tres años. Le gusta mucho jugar.

—Sí, eso es obvio.

—Armando, ¿qué tal si damos un paseo con Pepe? El pobre está muy triste. ¿Quieres?

—Sí, cómo no.

—¡Pepe! ¡Pepe!

—Mira, Raquel. La puerta está abierta.

—Ay no, Armando, Esta puerta siempre está cerrada. ¡Y Pepe no está aquí! ¡Pepe! ¡Pepe!

—¿Qué hacemos?

—Primero, llamar a Patricia. A veces Pepe va a su casa ya que vive cerca. Hola, Patricia... habla Raquel. Oye, ¿está Pepe en frente de tu casa? Okay... Patricia va a ver si Pepe está allí. ¿Cómo? ¿No está? Ay, qué lío. Muchísimas gracias, Patricia. Nos encontramos en la esquina en cinco minutos. Adiós. Patricia nos va a ayudar a buscar a Pepe.

—Muy bien. No te preocupes, Raquel. Vamos a encontrar a Pepe.

—Patricia, ven... ¿Cómo estás?

—¿Cómo estás?

—Otra vez lo mismo. Ese Pepe. Patricia, muchas gracias por ayudar a buscarlo.

—No hay de qué, Raquel. Oye, y José Luis lo va a buscar en la Calle Ocho para ayudarnos también.

—¡Qué bueno! Entonces en media hora nos encontramos aquí otra vez.

—Okay. Nos vemos.

—Bye.

—Gracias. ¿Usted ha visto un perro cobrador dorado?

—No, ay no, perdón. No lo he visto.

—Gracias.

—¡Pepe! ¡Pepe!

—¿Tú lo ves?

—No.

—¡Pepe!

—Buenas, ¿cómo estás?

—¿Has visto un perro por aquí?

—No.

—Es un *golden retriever*.

—¿No? Okay, gracias. Bye, bye.

—Disculpen.

—Gracias.

—¿Sí?

—Buscamos un perro perdido.

—¿Es grande o pequeño?

—Es bastante grande, de este tamaño más o menos. Es un perro cobrador dorado, muy bonito.

—Lo siento, pero no lo hemos visto. ¿Lleva collar?

—Sí, un collar azul con varias medallas de identificación.

—Eso va a ayudar mucho.

—Lo siento. Pero si lo vemos, ¿a quién llamamos?

—A la familia Suárez Camacho. Vivimos en la calle Bert y el número de teléfono está en la guía telefónica.

—Bien y buena suerte. ¡Ah! ¿Y cómo se llama tu perro?

—Se llama Pepe. ¡Muchas gracias!

—De nada.

—Bye.

—¿Y?

—Lo siento, Raquel, pero no lo vimos.

—Nosotros tampoco.

—Bueno, ¿quieren entrar?

—Sí.

—Okay, vamos.

—No te preocupes, Raquel. Pepe va a regresar. Los perros cobradores siempre regresan.

—Sobre todo cuando tienen hambre.

—Sí, tienen razón. Pero estoy muy preocupada.

—Oigan, ¿qué es eso?

—¡Pepe! ¡Pepe! ¡Pepe!

—Ven aquí, Pepe, ven aquí.

—Estuviste aquí el tiempo entero y nosotros buscándote por el barrio entero. ¡Ven acá! ¿Qué quieres ahora? ¿Dormir? ¡Qué perro tan perezoso eres, Pepe!

—¡Qué lindo!

Panorama cultural

In this chapter, we asked some people about their families and what they do to help around the house.

¿Cuántas personas hay en tu familia?

[Arantxa] Eh... somos cinco. Tengo dos hermanos menores. Cuando se van mis padres, me quedo con ellos en casa. Sí, tengo que ayudar en casa. Pues, ayudo a mi madre a recoger la casa y eso.

[Pablo] En mi familia hay cinco personas. Mi papá, mi mamá y mis dos hermanas. Yo lavo los platos, eh... limpio la cocina, arreglo mi cuarto y limpio mi baño.

[Brenda] Pues yo vivo en una familia de cinco y somos muy diferentes de los otros, pero tenemos cosas en comunes. Mi mamá es muy, muy protectiva, ¿no? Es muy cuidadosa de mí. Mi hermana es muy rebelde y nos peleamos mucho, este... pocas veces, pero nos llevamos bien y nos aconsejamos y somos como mejores amigas. Nos contamos secretos y nos confiamos en nosotros. Mi hermano es como un niño chiquito como son todos, que les gusta ah... hacerles cosas a los demás para este... darles problemas, dolores de cabeza, así como todos los niños chiquitos. Y mi papá es muy... como te diré, es muy, no le gusta reconocer muchas cosas, pero es muy bueno y les gusta cuidarnos mucho. Bueno, mi hermano no hace muchas cosas. La que hace más soy yo, porque mi mamá va al trabajo todos los días y viene cansada. Soy yo —como soy la más grande de los niños— yo los cuido y hago los trastes, este... trapeo.

[Éric] Somos siete: mis dos hermanas y tres hermanos. Tengo que ayudar a barrer el patio.

[Diego] Mi familia está compuesta eh... por cuatro personas. Somos mi mamá, mi papá, mi abuela y yo. Eh... los quehaceres del hogar los realiza mi madre y mi abuela.

[Angie] A ver, son cinco. Somos cinco personas en mi familia. Mi padrastro, mi mami, mi tía, mi hermano pequeño y yo. A veces sí, sí ayudo. Me considero una buena cocinera porque me gusta la cocina. ¿Y qué más? Arreglar la casa, mi pieza.

[Paola] En mi familia somos cuatro: mi mamá, mi papá y una hermana Luciana. Mi mamá, yo a veces la ayudo a hacer la comida, a lavar los platos, a limpiar, a hacer las camas.

Videoclips

¿Cierto que es muy bueno estar en familia? Porque en Antioquia es rico vivir. Cierto. ¡Cierto!

LOCATION OPENER:
Ecuador

Hola. Me llamo Diego Andrade y soy del Ecuador. Ésta es la ciudad de Quito. Qué belleza, ¿verdad? ¿Te gustaría ver más? Muy bien, ¡ven conmigo!

Ecuador, país de contrastes... País de montañas, selva y costa, de historia antigua y contemporánea, de lo indígena y lo europeo.

Quito, su hermosa capital, está situada al pie del volcán Pichincha. Quito es una ciudad en donde la arquitectura colonial y las construcciones modernas se complementan.

En las orillas del río Tomebamba se encuentra Cuenca... La conocida Catedral Nueva domina el parque central de esta ciudad colonial.

Las ruinas de las civilizaciones antiguas son testimonios de una larga historia... Muy conocidas son las ruinas de Ingapirca, construidas por los Incas hace más de quinientos años.

Las ricas culturas indígenas del Ecuador siguen manteniendo sus tradiciones... Un buen ejemplo son los habitantes del pueblo de Otavalo, famosos por sus textiles y su música.

Sin duda alguna, Ecuador es un país de contrastes... contrastes que armonizan para crear una sociedad dinámica y fascinante. Ecuador, joya de los Andes.

CAPÍTULO 7
¿Qué te gustaría hacer?

De antemano ¿Qué hacemos?

—¡Tomás! ¿Qué te pasa, Tomás? ¿Por qué estás de mal humor?

—María va a hacer una fiesta el sábado.

—¿Y? Me parece super bien.

—No me invitó.

—Qué lástima.

—Sí.

—Oye… ¿tienes prisa ahora? ¿Tienes que hacer algo?

—No, nada… ¿Por qué?

—¿Quieres ver un video en mi casa?

—¡Claro que sí! Vamos.

—Vamos.

—Oye, Tomás. Tengo una idea. ¿Te gustaría hacer algo conmigo este sábado? No tengo planes.

—Sí, por qué no.

—Hombre, qué entusiasmo. Bueno, ¿qué prefieres? ¿Salir o hacer algo en casa?

—En realidad, prefiero salir. Pero, ¿qué hacemos?

—Hay un concierto de guitarra en La Casa de la Cultura. ¿Tienes ganas de ir?

—Sí. ¡Buena idea!

—Muy bien entonces… El sábado vamos al concierto.

—¿Aló?

—Aló, ¿Carlos? Habla María.

—Ah… hola, María.

—Carlos, ¿quieres venir a una fiesta este sábado? Es para un estudiante de intercambio de Estados Unidos.

—¿Una fiesta? ¿El sábado? Eh… lo siento, María, pero no puedo. Ya tengo planes.

—Ay… qué lástima. ¿Seguro?

—Sí, lo siento.

—Bueno, tal vez otro día. Chao.

—Chao.

—Veamos la película.

—¿Aló?

—Buenas tardes, Sr. Ortiz. ¿Está Tomás, por favor?

—¿De parte de quién?

—Habla María Pérez.

—Hola, María… un momento.

—¡Tomás! ¡Tomás! ¡Teléfono! Lo siento, María, pero no está.

—Bueno. ¿Puedo dejar un recado, por favor?

—Claro que sí… pero un momento… Tengo que ponerme los lentes. A ver, María… ¿Sí?… fiesta… el sábado…

—Gracias. ¡Hasta luego!

—Muy bien. Chao, María.

—Hola, papi, ¿cómo estás?

—Hola, mi amor. ¿Cómo te fue?

—Bien.

—¿Me ayudas un momentito?

—Claro que sí.

¿Qué hacemos? (a continuación)

—Buenas tardes, Sr. Ortiz.

—Hola. ¿Cómo te va, María?

—Bien, gracias.

—¡Tomás! ¡Tomás!

—¡Voy!

—Hola, Tomás!

—Hola, ¿qué tal?

—Bien, gracias. Oye, ¿vienes a la fiesta?

—¿Cómo?

—La fiesta… el sábado. Dejé el recado con tu papá. ¿No te lo dijo? Bueno, te explico. Este sábado voy a hacer una fiesta. El viernes llega un estudiante de Estados Unidos que viene a vivir con nosotros durante un mes. Se llama Hiroshi y queremos hacerle una fiesta de bienvenida. ¿Te gustaría venir a la fiesta?

—Sí, claro. Me gustaría mucho. ¡Gracias!

—¡Perfecto! Entonces, a las cuatro, en mi casa. ¿Está bien?

—Sí, a las cuatro.

—Bueno, chao.

—Chao.

—La fiesta… la fiesta… ¡el sábado! Ay, no… el concierto de guitarra…Tengo que llamar a Carlos.

—¡Chuza! ¡La línea está ocupada!

—Tomás, ¿Como estás?

—Hola, te estaba llamando.

—Ah, ¿sí?

—Tengo que hablar contigo.

—Y… ¿de qué?

—Quiero ir contigo al concierto…

—Sí, va a estar buenazo.

—Pero, es que… Resulta que María sí me invitó a su fiesta. Es que habló con mi papá y yo no lo sabía. De verdad, tengo muchas ganas de ir a la fiesta. Lo siento, Carlos.

—¿Cómo? ¿La fiesta de María? Tomás… Bueno, pues, esto es fácil de arreglar. Como María también me invitó a mí, yo la puedo volver a llamar y aceptar su invitación. Podemos ir juntos a la fiesta entonces. ¿Qué te parece?

—¡Perfecto!

—¡Hola! ¿Qué tal?

—Hola.

—¡Aquí estamos!

—Sí… aquí están… ¿y? Pero… ¿no saben?

—¿Qué?

—¿Mi mamá no los llamó?

—No.

—Ay, lo siento mucho… Es que Hiroshi no llega hasta el lunes. Vamos a hacer la fiesta el próximo fin de semana. Ay, lo siento mucho.

—Está bien, María. No te preocupes. ¿Pero qué hacemos ahora, Carlos?

—No sé. Ya es tarde para ir al concierto.

—Bueno, yo no tengo planes para esta tarde. ¿Por qué no hacemos algo? Podemos dar una vuelta a pie y tomar algo. Yo los invito.

—Sí, perfecto.

Capítulo 7 *cont.*

—Un momento. Necesito ponerme una chaqueta, peinarme y luego vamos.
—Gracias.
—Oye, María. ¿Cómo es Hiroshi? ¿Lo conoces desde hace mucho?
—No, sólo sé que es un chico de 17 años y es de San Francisco, California. Sus padres son de Japón y viene aquí porque es parte de un programa de intercambio con nuestro colegio. Este año él viene aquí a Quito y el próximo año yo me voy a San Francisco.
—¿A San Francisco? ¡Qué chévere! ¿Cuánto tiempo vas?
—Por un mes también.
—¿Y es la primera vez que Hiroshi viene al Ecuador?
—Sí, es la primera vez. Vamos a enseñarle todo Quito.
—Le va a encantar. Es una maravilla.
—Sí.
—Entonces, María. ¿Cuándo va a ser la fiesta?
—Uy, qué vergüenza. Lo siento, de verdad.
—Ah, María, no importa. No te preocupes más.
—Bueno, el próximo sábado, a las cuatro. ¿Pueden venir?
—Yo sí.
—Yo también. Pero si hay cambio de planes, nos vas a llamar tú. ¿No es cierto?
—¡Sí, lo prometo!

Panorama cultural

How would you ask someone out in a Spanish-speaking country? Who would pay for the date? We asked these students to tell us about dating customs in their countries.

¿Qué haces para conocer a una persona?

[Rodrigo] Ah... me le acerco, le pregunto su nombre, me presento y le pido su número telefónico o algo así. Los hombres pagamos la cita en Ecuador.

[Jessica] Busco una persona amiga mía que me la presente. Él... él siempre paga la cita.

[María Isabel] Trato de que me lo presenten, y una vez que me lo presentan, pues... trato de tener conversación con él. No nos dejan pagar. Pero... me gusta que me inviten, pero yo también quiero, o sea, que me gusta invitar a mí también.

[María Luisa] Bueno, pido que me presenten y ya de allí converso con él y veo si es que realmente me gusta o no. Depende si son enamorados, o si es que ya se te va a declarar, salen solos, o si no salen en grupo.

[Manolo] Este... cuando conozco una muchacha bonita que no conozco y me gustaría conocerla, casi siempre pues hago como que si estoy caminando en, en el pasillo. Hago como que me tropiezo o algo, le rozo tantito y digo, ¡Ay! perdón. Perdóneme y sale la plática y comenzamos a platicar. Me gusta... cuando salgo con una chica, me gusta salir solo con ella. Podemos platicar de cosas de ella y cosas mías, sin, sin que me dé vergüenza de las otras gentes, de otras personas que van junto conmigo.

[Siria] Le digo que lo llevo a dar una vuelta y le digo que cómo está, vamos a salir. Si es extranjero, le enseño los lugares de Costa Rica.

[Ixchel] Um... le pregunto cualquier cosa para llamar la atención, ¿no? La mayoría de veces, ellos, se supone. Pero... cuando no, cada quien paga lo suyo.

[Carlos] Bueno, yo si quiero conocer a una chica, primero le pregunto su nombre, le digo cuál es su edad y nos conocemos mutuamente. La cita la pagamos la mayoría de veces entre todos y cuesta alrededor de unos mil colones.

Videoclips

—Ve. ¿Y qué será de Miguel?
—¿Y sigue viviendo en Bogotá?
—¿Por qué no lo llamamos?
—¡Ay no! Es muy maluco con Magaly.
—Qué le hace.
—Qué le hace, llamémosle.
—¡Aló! Miguel, llamamos a saludarte. Anda por Magaly.
—¡Magaly! ¡Magaly!
En esta Navidad EDA le regala el 50% de descuento en sus llamadas de larga distancia nacional, de siete de la noche a siete de la mañana. EDA comunica a los antioqueños con el mundo.

CAPÍTULO 8
¡A comer!

De antemano ¿Qué vas a pedir?

—Ay, ¿tienes hambre, Hiroshi?

—Ah, sí. Tengo mucha hambre. Ya es la una y media y por lo general almuerzo a las doce.

—No te preocupes, Hiroshi. Vas a comer bien en el restaurante. Para el almuerzo hay platos especiales típicos de la región andina. Mm… vamos.

—¡Qué linda vista!, ¿no?
¿Qué vas a pedir?

—Eh…. No sé… ¿qué van a pedir ustedes?

—Mm… creo que voy a pedir el sancocho. Pero el locro es delicioso aquí también.

—¿Qué son ésos? ¿Son sopas?

—Sí, mira allí en esa mesa. Ellos comen locro. Es una sopa de papas, queso, y aguacate **(palta?)*****

—Buenas tardes. ¿Qué les puedo traer?

—Buenas tardes.

—Para mí, el sancocho, por favor.

—El sancocho está bien, pero a mí me encantan las empanadas. Empanadas, por favor.

—Muy bien. Empanadas para la señorita.

—Uyf, no me gustan para nada las empanadas.

—¿Me trae carne colorada con papas, por favor?

—Cómo no, señor. ¿Y para usted, joven?

—Eh… quisiera locro, por favor.

—¿Y para tomar? ¿Nos trae cuatro aguas?

—Sí. En seguida se lo traigo.

—Saben, tengo mucha hambre.

—¡Cuidado Hiroshi, eso es ají! Es muy picante. No le pongas mucho.

—Ay, ay, ay, ay, ay ay. ¡Está picante! En casa no como mucha comida picante. ¡Necesito agua! Ah, aquí viene.

—¿Qué es?

—Esto es ají. Tienes que tener cuidado. Es un condimento de cebolla, chile y tomate. Puedes comer un poco de ají con pan, pero tienes que tener cuidado, eh.

—Hiroshi, ¿te gusta el locro?

—Sí, María, me gusta mucho. Por lo general como mucha sopa en casa. Por eso me encanta.

—¿Cuánto es?

—A ver… son veintidós dólares con ochenta. Pero la propina es aparte. ¡Yo los invito!

—Gracias.

—¿Y ahora?

—¡A la Mitad del Mundo! Vamos…

—¡Ay, no!

—Increíble.

—Y ahora, ¿qué?

—Muchas gracias por ayudarnos, señor.

—Pues, no hay de qué. Que les vaya bien. Buen viaje.

—Adiós. Hasta luego. Gracias. Adiós. Hasta luego.

—¡Vamos! Sólo nos quedan dos horas y hay mucho que ver. Te va a gustar mucho el Monumento de la Mitad del Mundo, Hiroshi.

—¿Te gustan los tapices?

—Sí. Me gustan muchísimo, sobre todo éste. ¿Cuánto cuesta?

—Depende. Tienes que regatear el precio con el vendedor. Mira. Buenas tardes, señor.

—Buenas tardes, señorita.

—¿Cuánto cuesta este tapiz?

—Este hermoso tapiz le cuesta veinticinco dólares.

—Señor, es un tapiz muy bonito, pero ¿veinticinco dólares? Es un precio bastante alto. Le damos diez dólares.

—No, señorita, no puedo. El último precio que le puedo ofrecer es veinte dólares.

—¿Me lo deja en quince dólares?

—Está bien.

—¿Ves? Es muy fácil. Y toma. Es un regalo.

—¿En serio, María? ¡Muchas gracias!

—Buenas tardes. A la orden.

—Buenas tardes.

—Buenas tardes. A la orden.

—Quiero comprar un suéter de lana para mi hermana.

—¿De qué tamaño?

—Ah… no sé.

—¿Qué le parece éste?

—¡Uy! Es demasiado grande.

—¿Y éste?

—¡No! Es demasiado pequeño.

—Uy, qué pena.

—¿Y éste?

—Quiero comprar ése.

—Muy bien, joven. Éste se lo doy por veinte dólares.

—Es mucho, señor, pero le puedo dar doce dólares. .

—No puedo joven. Le voy a hacer un precio muy especial… Se lo dejo en dieciocho dólares.

—Mm… quince dólares.

—Bueno.

—Gracias.

—Hasta luego.

—Hasta luego.

—Que les vaya bien.

—¿Qué tal? ¿La pasaron bien?

—Sí, pasamos un día increíble.

—¿Qué compraron? ¿Compraron muchas cosas?

—Bueno, María me compró este tapiz. Muy amable. Muchas gracias de nuevo, María.

—No, no hay de qué, Hiroshi.

—Qué bonito. ¿Qué más compraron?

—A ver. Yo compré esta bufanda… y un suéter para mi hermana.

—Son muy lindos. Seguro que a tu hermana le va a encantar el suéter.

—Sí, y fíjense que aprendió muy rápido a regatear los precios con los vendedores.

—Muy bien. Bien por ti Hiroshi.

—Bueno chicos, se nos hace tarde. Ya tenemos que irnos. ¿Listos?

—Sí, estamos listos, pero antes… ¡yo voy a ver si hay suficiente gasolina en el tanque!

Panorama cultural

There are as many different "typical" dishes in the Spanish-speaking world as there are countries and regions. In this chapter we asked people to tell us about the dishes typical to their areas.

¿Cuál es un plato típico de tu país o región?

[Diana] Un plato típico…, plátanos maduros, con, con bistec empanizado. Tiene un bistec que está cocinado en pan y un poco de arroz, unos plátanos que están cocinados con, con azúcar.

[Héctor] El pabellón. Es un plato que contiene arroz, caráota, carne mechada y tajada. Es el plato típico de Venezuela.

[Juan Fernando] El huevo frito con llapingachos y lechuga. Es uno de los platos más típicos que hay, que se inventó cuando vino la colonia española acá, ya que ellos no comían nada de lo preparado por los indígenas. Así que los sembríos de papa y tomate y yuca se prepararon estos… este plato, de allí salió. Este plato lo comían los mineros en la época colonial. Llapingachos son tortillas de papa con queso.

[Sra. González] ¿De aquí? La tortilla española, el gazpacho andaluz, qué más te diría. ¿La tortilla española? De muchas maneras. Se le echa de todo: pimiento, cebolla, ajo, todo lo que le quieras echar, más buena está.

[Maria] Ajiaco colombiano. ¿Qué lleva? Pollo, eh… papa, emm… maíz, de todo, todo.

[Rodrigo] ¿Plato típico? Eh… un plato típico vendría a ser asado, porque acá a los argentinos nos gusta mucho la carne y somos fanáticos de lo que sea todo vacuno y esas cosas. El asado es carne,

es una parte de la vaca, que es allá la costilla, digamos, y nos gusta mucho porque ¡bah! siempre la comemos. Es nuestra comida preferida, ¿no? de los argentinos.

[Gisela] Yo creo que ya Venezuela no tiene platos típicos. Como dije es una mezcla de muchos países, de muchas inmigraciones, de mucha gente. Entonces hay platos típicos ya también es la pasta. Plato típico ya también es la hamburguesa. Plato típico también es un sándwich. Ya no se puede hablar de un plato típico en Venezuela, ¿no? Es una mezcla de todo.

[Ema] Un plato típico puede ser el mole, platillo de mole, enchiladas, el pollo asado… Em, este… Las enchiladas se hacen con tortilla, pollo, queso, crema, este… verduras y… la salsa.

[Sr. Rosado] Aquí tienen el plato más típico que hay en Puerto Rico. Unas Navidades sin gandules no son Navidades en Puerto Rico. Esto se usa mucho en Puerto Rico, especialmente ahora en los días navideños y éste es un grano que aquí es caro, porque es un grano que escasea por tiempo. Y es un grano que es muy rico en hierro, sí, y es el plato típico de Puerto Rico.

[Raquel] Nacatamal. Es un plato muy típico de Nicaragua. Se hace con… tiene masa, tiene arroz, y son como los tamales cubanos —no sé si ustedes los habrán probado, los tamales cubanos —y tiene chancho adentro.

Videoclips

[Leche Ram]
Estos angelitos han descubierto ya la leche vitaminada Ram y su profesor aún no lo sabe. Para niños en plena forma, leche vitaminada Ram enriquecida con vitaminas. Energía inagotable.

[Dos Pinos]
—¿Sabes?
—Sí, sabes. ¡Ooh!
Néctares Dos Pinos, ¡verdadero sabor!

[La Casera]
—¡Paren máquinas! Hombre a borda. Corriendo. Volando, volando. Ánimo hombre.
—Para habernos matado. Qué hambre he pasado. Dios mío.
—Comida, comida para este hombre. Rápido. Rápido, comida para este hombre.
—Comida, comida.
—Ya ha pasado todo, hijo.
—Y la Casera.
—Tráigale una Casera.
—Una Casera.
—Pero vaya Ud. comiendo.
—Es que yo sin Casera no.
—Y la Casera marchando. Ya vamos.

—No, es que yo sin la Casera no como.
—Pero, hombre, coma.
—Que no, y ya está.
La Casera. No coma sin ella.

LOCATION OPENER:
Texas

¡Hola! Me llamo Gabi y éstas son mis amigas Lisa y Eva. Somos de San Antonio, Texas. San Antonio es una ciudad fascinante. Estamos ahora en el Mercado. ¿Quieres ver más? Muy bien, ¡ven conmigo!

Texas es el segundo estado más grande y más poblado de los Estados Unidos. Seis banderas han ondeado sobre Texas, incluyendo las de España y México...

La Misión de San José en San Antonio... buen ejemplo de la vida colonial española de hace doscientos años.

El pasado hispano de Texas vive aún en los nombres: San Antonio... El Paso... el río Guadalupe... la Isla del Padre...

La herencia mexicana también se encuentra en las comidas, la música y las fiestas.

San Antonio, donde más de la mitad de la población es mexicoamericana. Millones de visitantes llegan cada año a visitar sus atracciones.

El Paseo del Río, con sus cafés al aire libre en el centro de la ciudad...

La Plaza del Mercado, con sus tiendas y restaurantes típicos.

Texas, por su historia, su diversidad y su aire mexicano, es un estado ¡sin igual!

CAPÍTULO 9
¡Vamos de compras!

De antemano
¿Qué le compramos a Héctor?

—Bueno, ¿qué le van a comprar a Héctor para su graduación?
—No sé, tal vez unos discos compactos de Gloria Estefan.
—Me gustaría regalarle algo divertido.
—Gabi, ¡yo también quiero regalarle algo divertido!
—¿Por qué no le compran regalos divertidos las dos? Pero tenemos que encontrarlos hoy. ¡Su fiesta de graduación es el viernes!
—Bueno, sí, vamos.
—¿Quieren entrar a esta tienda de ropa para mirar, nada más, y después vamos a la papelería para comprarle a Héctor las tarjetas?
—Sí, vamos.
—Sí, está bien.
—¿Cuál prefieren, la blusa roja o la de rayas?
—Yo prefiero la roja. ¿Cuánto cuesta?
—Ay, cuarenta dólares. Es cara.
—¿Qué les parecen estos pantalones cortos?
—Eh... de verdad, Lisa, no me gustan para nada los cuadros.
—Qué tal éstos. Mira.
—¡Lisa! ¡Eva! ¿Qué tal esta falda?
—Es bonita...
—Y es de algodón...
—Y sólo cuesta 12 dólares. ¡Qué barata!
—Sí, ¡es una ganga! Pero no la voy a comprar hoy. Hoy tenemos que comprarle regalos a Héctor.
—Bueno, ¿qué le compramos a Héctor?
—Uf... Es difícil... No sé... Le interesan los libros. ¿Tal vez un libro? Hay una librería al lado de la zapatería.
—No, eso no. Prefiero regalarle algo divertido.
—Vamos a ver quién le compra el regalo más divertido. ¿Por qué no vas a buscar algo y yo voy también? Y nos vemos aquí en... ¿media hora?
—Yo voy a buscar algo también. Muy bien, hasta luego. Aquí en media hora.
—Ay, llevo éste.
—Muchas gracias.
—De nada.
—Ay, mira, quiero éste.
—Aquí.
—Bueno.
—Quiero éste.
—Aquí.
—Bueno.

¿Qué le compramos a Héctor?
(a continuación)

—¡Ah! Aquí están.

—Por fin.

—¡Hola! Oigan, ¿por qué no vamos a la nueva joyería? Dicen que tiene anillos muy bonitos y a un buen precio además.

—Perfecto.

—Sí, vamos.

—Vamos.

—¡Vengan! ¡Miren qué bonito!

—¡Ese anillo es precioso!

—¿Cuál? ¿El grande?

—No, no... el que está a la derecha del grande, el anillo con el amatista.

—Ah, sí. Es muy bonito pero yo prefiero el anillo de plata, al lado, y esos aretes me gustan muchísimo.

—Vámonos.

—Disculpe. ¿Sabe usted por qué está aquí un mariachi? ¿Qué pasa? ¿Hay una boda?

—No, es que hay un festival de música mexicana y tejana en San Antonio este fin de semana. Debe ser un grupo de los que están aquí para el festival. Son muy buenos, ¿verdad?

—Sí, muchas gracias.

—Gabi, bailas muy bien.

—Gracias, pero es el señor que baila bien. ¡Qué energía!

—¿Verdad?

—Bueno... ¿qué tienen para Héctor? ¿Son regalos divertidos?

—Sí, le va a encantar. Es un cartel muy divertido.

—Ay, no, yo también tengo un cartel para Héctor y parece que tú tienes un cartel también, Eva.

—Sí, pero no importa. Así tiene muchas cosas para poner en su cuarto.

—Abre tu cartel también, Gabi.

—Miren. Es divertido, ¿verdad?

—Lisa, mira.

—Ay, Gabi, tenemos el mismo cartel.

—Y no sólo ustedes, pero yo también.

—¿Qué hacemos?

—Mira, bueno yo aquí tengo dos discos compactos. Yo puedo devolver este cartel.

—Y hay otro cartel que me gusta también en la misma tienda. Puedo devolver este cartel y comprar el otro y tú le regalas a Héctor éste, Lisa.

—¿Seguro?

—Sí, no te preocupes. Está bien. Vamos. Regresamos a la tienda.

—Está bien.

—Sí, vamos.

Panorama cultural

Hispanic teens usually try to look as fashionable as they possibly can. Much of what is popular in the United States is also in style in Spain and Latin America. But what counts is quality, not quantity. Here are some comments from teenagers about what is usually **de moda** and what's definitely not.

¿Estás a la moda?

[Soledad] Yo cuando voy a una fiesta me pongo un vestido ajustado. Lo importante es uno mismo y uno mismo nunca pasa de moda.

[Gisela] Bueno, depende de la fiesta, pero una fiesta de mis amigos normalmente como estoy ahorita, ¿no? Un vestido, bluejeans. No, no, no es tan importante. Es más la ropa que me guste, más que la moda. No toda la moda me queda bien.

[Pablo] Bueno, a como amerite. Si es en el campo, vamos de sport y si es algo ya formal, nos ponemos traje. Claro que sí, es andar en la actualidad con todos, ¿verdad? No quedarse atrás.

[Yaremi] Está de moda la ropa típica de los años 60 con las botas anchas, los suecos, este... también las camisas que tienen la, o sea la manga larga, también ancha. Y bueno eso es lo que más o menos se lleva. A veces uno se viste más de moda cuando va a lugares nocturnos, o simplemente para estar casi igual a los demás. Pero para estar a diario en la calle, no, no es necesario.

[Rodrigo] Y siempre trato de vestirme formal, bien, para estar presentable para la gente. Y sí para estar de moda para, para adelantarnos un poco, ¿no?

[Gretel] No, no es importante. Yo creo que, bah, yo no me visto a la moda sino más bien lo que yo tengo ganas de ponerme ese día y este, y... casi todo el mundo va, este, de negro, ahora. O sea la moda es irse de negro y yo no sé, pero yo no me pongo eso. No me gusta estar a la moda.

[Cindy] Lo adecuado, depende de la ocasión. Si es este... entre jóvenes, este, un jeans y una camiseta basta; y si es así, más seria, por decirlo así, entonces un vestido. La moda sólo, sólo es artificial. Lo que más importa es la persona adentro.

[Johnny] Me visto sencillo. No hay que estar tan, tan llamativo. Para mí no es tanto el estar de moda sino sentirme yo, nada más.

[Gala] Me pongo jeans, borceguíes, y me pongo alguna camisa o si no... Pero eso es para ir a bailar, cuando voy a bailar acá con mis amigas. Si no, me puedo poner un vestido, no sé. Bah, no sé si es importante pero, pero me gusta estar a la moda porque me gusta estar más... me gusta sentirme que estoy bien vestida y además porque me gusta. Si no me gusta no lo uso.

[Jaharlyn] Cuando voy a una fiesta depende del tipo de fiesta que sea. Si es una fiesta pues donde... una boda, una celebración bien importante, pues uso ropa fina. Si es una fiesta entre los amigos, pues uso ropa casual. Si la ropa que está de moda me gusta, pues si la uso y si no, pues no la compro.

Videoclips

Bienvenidos a 2 x 1, la verdadera tienda de departamentos de Costa Rica. Traemos artículos de todo el mundo a un lugar acogedor. Con personal amable, amplios pasillos y secciones especializadas. No tenemos intermediarios. Por eso lo conseguimos todo a precios justos porque queremos que Ud. siempre salga ganando. Esto es: 2 x 1, la verdadera tienda de departamentos de Costa Rica donde Ud. siempre sale ganando.

CAPÍTULO 10
Celebraciones

De antemano
¡Felicidades Héctor!

—¡Tomás!
—¿Sí?
—Mira, ¿qué te parece?
—¡Perfecto! Oye, Marcela, ¿dónde están los globos?
—No sé. Pregúntale a Juan.
—¡Juan! ¿Tienes los globos?
—Sí, aquí están.
—¿Me ayudas a inflarlos?
—¡Claro que sí, papá! ¿Y qué tal si usamos de todos los colores? Hay de violeta, rojo, azul y verde...
—Buena idea. Empecemos.
—Sí, sí. El apellido es Villarreal, Manuel Villarreal. Es un pastel para mi hijo, Héctor. Es para su graduación de la escuela secundaria. Sí, de chocolate. Ah, muy bien. ¿Cómo? Hmm... un momento... ¡Rebeca! Estoy hablando con un empleado de la pastelería. ¿Qué escribimos en el pastel?
—¿Cuántas palabras podemos escribir?
—¿Cuántas palabras pueden escribir? Ajá... un momento, por favor. Es un pastel bastante grande. Pueden escribir muchas.

—Entonces, pon "Felicidades en el día de tu graduación, Héctor".
—Entonces, ponga "Felicidades en el día de tu graduación, Héctor". Gracias.
—Eva, ¿me pasas las hojas?
—Sí, abuelita.
—Gracias.
—Preparar tamales es mucho trabajo, ¿no?
—Pero es la comida favorita de Héctor. Generalmente, sólo preparamos muchos tamales en diciembre, para la Navidad. Es una tradición de la cultura mexicana.
—¿Hay tradiciones mexicanas para otros días festivos también?
—Claro que sí. Hay muchas. Durante las Pascuas, sobre todo en Semana Santa, hay desfiles. En el Día de la Independencia, que es el 16 de septiembre, hay fuegos artificiales. Pero mi día festivo favorito es el Día de los Muertos. Me acuerdo de un año en particular...
—¿Qué hiciste, abuela?
—Pues, lo de siempre. Mi mamá preparó comida para llevar a la tumba de la familia y yo ayudé también. Ese año, yo compré comida en la pequeña tienda cerca de la casa, pero pasó algo especial...
—Manuel... ¡Manuel! ¿Qué son éstos, hermano?
—Ah... son las invitaciones. ¡Las invitaciones! ¡No mandé las invitaciones!

¡Felicidades Héctor!
(a continuación)

—¡Qué desastre! ¡No mandé las invitaciones! ¿Qué hacemos? La fiesta comienza en dos horas? ¡Ay, no! Mira. Tengo todavía las invitaciones. No las mandé.
—Manuel, es un problema, pero no te preocupes. Todavía tenemos tiempo para llamar por teléfono a los invitados y muchos ya están aquí.
—Sí, sí... Es verdad...
—Muy bien, voy a llamar a todos, pero no de aquí. Voy a la habitación. Si me necesitas, allí estoy.
—Qué lío... Bueno, ni modo. Adelante con las decoraciones.
—¿Cómo va la piñata, compadre?
—Ahí vamos, compadrito.
—Bueno, mamá. ¿Cómo va todo?
—Todo va muy bien. Ya casi terminamos. ¿Y las decoraciones?
—Ya está todo.
—Qué bueno.
—¿Eva?
—¿Sí, papá?
—Eva, ¿me haces un favor? El pastel ya debe estar listo. ¿Puedes ir a la pastelería por el pastel? Te doy el dinero.
—Claro que sí, papá. La pastelería está en la calle San Pedro, ¿verdad?

—Sí.

—Okay.

—¿Por qué no van las muchachas con Eva a la pastelería? Ya casi está terminado aquí y no necesito a nadie y si necesito ayuda pues aquí está Francisco.

—Bueno, adiós abuelita.

—Adiós. Hasta luego.

—Hola, muchachas. Buenos días.

—Hola, buenas tardes. ¿El pastel para Villarreal?

—Un momento, por favor.

—Héctor no sabe nada de la fiesta, ¿verdad?

—No creo... pero con tantas preparaciones, debe sospechar algo.

—¿Y cuándo sale a la universidad? Va a ir a UCLA, ¿verdad?

—Va a trabajar aquí en San Antonio durante el verano y sale para Los Ángeles a finales de agosto.

—El pastel está aquí.

—El pastel ya llegó.

—Debe ser bonito.

—Sí, debe de ser bien bonito.

—¡No!

—¡Apúrenle! Ustedes están acá detrás.

—¿A qué hora llega Héctor a la casa?

—Pronto. Trabaja hasta las tres y después toma el autobús. Entonces debe llegar a las tres y media. Ya son las dos y media. Tenemos que regresar rápido.

—¡Es Héctor!

—¡Pero trabaja hasta las tres!

—Hmmm. Obviamente, hoy no.

—¡Pero no puede llegar a la casa todavía! Tengo que hacer algo. Miren. Vayan a la casa y expliquen lo que pasa.

—Pero, ¿qué vas a hacer?

—No sé todavía. ¡Vayan! Héctor no nos puede ver juntas.

—¡Héctor! ¡Héctor!

—¡Eva! ¿Qué haces aquí?

—Nada. Mamá me mandó a un mandado, nomás aquí a la calle.

—Ah, bienvenidos. Entren, entren.

—¿Llegamos tarde?

—No, no... Héctor y Eva todavía no están. Pasen al patio.

—¡Aquí vienen! ¡Aquí vienen! Ahora, cuando entren, silencio total, ¿está bien?

—¡Felicidades!

—Eso, hijo mío. ¡Muchas felicidades!

—Gracias, mamá. Gracias, papá. Oye, pero trabajaron muchísimo para organizar todo esto.

—Ah, no de ninguna manera. No tuvimos ningún problema. ¿Verdad, Rebeca?

—¿Eh? ¿Problemas? No, no. Todo fue muy fácil. ¿Verdad, hijita?

—¿Mande?

—Tuvimos mucha ayuda.

Panorama cultural

Festivals are a very important part of life in Spanish-speaking countries. Often the whole community participates. Here is how some people celebrate holidays in their communities.

¿Qué hacen ustedes para celebrar?

[Sra. Pardo] Eh... es la fiesta de la Virgen del Rosario. Es una fiesta eminentemente religiosa. Bueno, la música tradicionales, hay bailes, eh, típicos gallegos, como la muñeira, y luego canciones, música popular gallega, de origen celta, fundamentalmente.

[Angélica] Bueno, el 5 de julio que se celebra la batalla de Carabobo. Eso se celebra en los Próceres que es un parque que queda cerca. Este, todos los militares salen a desfilar. Sale la Armada, la Aviación, el Ejército y la Guardia. Eso fue por la... para la indepen... cuando hubo la independencia de Carabobo, del estado de Carabobo.

[Verónica] El 16 de septiembre significa la Independencia de México y cuando tenemos una celebración del 16 de septiembre en, bueno en Laredo, tenemos como un baile. Porque significa más la independencia de Mexico y si México no hubiera ganado su independencia de España nunca estuviéramos nosotros aquí, los hispanos, aquí donde estamos hoy.

[Claudia] El carnaval se celebra con comparsa, este calipso, que es el baile que se baila, el calipso, este, disfraces.

[Carlo Magno] Todos los años el 15 de septiembre, escuelas, colegios, universidades y el pueblo en general, celebra con gran alegría la fecha de la Independencia Patria, así la llamamos. En los últimos años se trae lo que se llama la antorcha de la libertad que atraviesa toda Centroamérica. Nosotros la recibimos en la frontera con Nicaragua. Los estudiantes la van trayendo, la van trayendo. Aquí en Heredia, donde estamos, casualmente en este parque, el 14 de septiembre a las cuatro o cinco de la tarde llega. Luego continúa rumbo a San José hasta llegar a Cartago que era la antigua capital nuestra. Los colegios hacen sus asambleas respectivas. En los lugares céntricos se hacen desfiles. Aquí desfilan todos los colegios con su bandera de Costa Rica tricolor: el blanco, azul y rojo.

[Ana María] El 24 de mayo que es la batalla de Pichincha. Hay desfiles de los militares por las avenidas más importantes de aquí del Ecuador, en honor a los militares que defendieron hace tiempos.

[Elena y Blanca] Pues la Virgen del Sagrario se celebra el 15 de agosto y el Corpus se celebraría, pero se suele celebrar en junio. Pues hay una procesión, se adornan las calles y pues la gente sale a las calles a verlas y a pasear.

[Ignacio] Celebramos cuando se inauguró la ciudad, cuando se hizo la ciudad. Se celebra con toros. Eh... yo creo que ésta es mi fiesta favorita, porque toda la gente está muy feliz, todo está, está chévere.

Videoclips

¿Cierto que Navidad todos queremos estar juntos? Aunque no puedas estar en casa, ¡feliz Navidad! Cierto. ¡Cierto!

LOCATION OPENER: Puerto Rico

Hola, ¿qué tal? Yo me llamo Benjamín y ella es mi hermana Carmen. Somos puertorriqueños pero vivimos en Nueva York. Ahora estamos en Puerto Rico, en la capital, San Juan. Puerto Rico es una isla hermosa. ¿Te gustaría ver más? Muy bien, ¡ven con nosotros!

Puerto Rico, isla de grandes bellezas naturales...

San Juan, su encantadora capital, es una de las ciudades españolas más antiguas en las Américas.

En el Viejo San Juan se encuentra el Castillo San Felipe del Morro, una fortaleza construida en el siglo dieciséis por los españoles...

Hoy, San Juan es un importante destino turístico con sus monumentos históricos y playas atractivas.

Además... El Yunque, un bosque espectacular... es el refugio de muchas especies de animales raros...

Ponce es la segunda ciudad más grande de Puerto Rico. Los ponceños están muy orgullosos de su espléndida ciudad y la llaman "La Perla del Sur".

Los edificios de colores pasteles hacen juego con las flores multicolores de Puerto Rico... isla de encantos.

CAPÍTULO 11
Para vivir bien

De antemano
Un recorrido por San Juan

—¡Mamá! ¡Mira! ¡Hay palmeras por todas partes! ¡Y mira! ¡Los edificios son de tantos colores bonitos!
—Sí, Carmen, hay muchas palmeras en Puerto Rico. Y tienes razón, los edificios son de muchos colores.
—Mamá, ¿y por qué allá en Nueva York no tenemos edificios de tantos colores bonitos como aquí?
—Pues, no sé. Cada parte del mundo tiene costumbres diferentes, y aquí en el Caribe, es costumbre pintar los edificios de muchos colores. Nueva York no es así.
—Puerto Rico es muy bonito. ¡Qué bien pasar aquí las vacaciones!
—Verdad. Pero para mí, la mejor parte es pasarla con tu abuelo y nuestra familia aquí. Ay, es tan difícil estar tan lejos de ellos, allá en Nueva York.
—Sí, abuelito está muy contento de tenernos aquí, ¿verdad?
—Sí, es verdad.
—Bueno, hijos. Aquí estamos en la Plaza de Armas. A las tres paso por ustedes por la Plaza de Hostos y después vamos al partido de béisbol de su tío, ¿de acuerdo?
—Sí, mamá. Carmen y yo te esperamos en la Plaza de Hostos a las tres.
—Bueno, entonces, hasta las tres. Vamos. ¡Que la pasen bien!
—Adiós, mamá.
—Hasta luego.
—¡Vamos! Tenemos todo el día para explorar el Viejo San Juan y hace muy buen tiempo. ¿Tienes ganas de caminar?
—Ay, sí, venga.
—Ben, me duelen los pies. Estoy cansada. ¿Podemos descansar? Caminamos mucho.
—Claro, Carmen. Yo también tengo ganas de descansar. A mí me duelen los pies. ¿Por qué no descansamos en esta banca? Pero mira. Ya es la una y media. No tenemos mucho tiempo. ¿Qué tienes ganas de ver ahora?
—Hola. gracias.
—De nada. Hola. Tú ¿eres de San Juan?
—Sí, y ustedes, ¿no son de aquí, verdad?
—No. Somos de Nueva York.
—Estamos en Puerto Rico de vacaciones. Estamos visitando a nuestra familia de aquí.
—Yo tengo familia en Nueva York. Una tía, creo. Pues miren, yo me llamo Pedro, Pedro Méndez.
—Yo soy Benjamín Corredor, pero me llaman Ben y ésta es mi hermana.

—Carmen. Me llamo Carmen.

—Mucho gusto. ¿Adónde van ahora?

—Bueno, ya fuimos a la Puerta de San Juan y al museo de Pablo Casals.

—Ay, yo tengo ganas de ir a ver el Castillo del Morro. ¿Podemos?

—¿Qué tal si yo los acompaño? A mí me gusta mucho el Castillo del Morro.

—Sí, perfecto. Vamos al Castillo del Morro.

—¿Juegan mucho al béisbol en Nueva York?

—Sí, bastante. Aquí también juegan mucho al béisbol, ¿verdad? Mi tío que vive aquí juega muy bien al béisbol.

—¡No me digas! Mi tío es un excelente jugador de béisbol también.

—¡Mira!

—¿Juegas algún otro deporte? ¿Qué más te gusta hacer?

—Bueno, a mí me gusta patinar sobre ruedas— como ese muchacho que va por ahí.

—¿Ah, sí? ¿Patinas sobre hielo también?

—Yo sí, a veces, pero no me gusta el frío porque cuando hace frío, ay, me duele la nariz y también me duelen las orejas.

—Una vez fui a una pista de patinaje. Es difícil pero me gustó mucho. Mira, el Castillo. Vamos allá.

—¡Uf! Estoy cansada. ¿Podemos descansar? Aquí hay un muro.

—Pues, Carmen, es que estás corriendo mucho. ¿Te gusta el Castillo del Morro? Oye, aquí en el panfleto dice que comenzaron la construcción en mil quinientos treinta y nueve.

—¿En mil quinientos treinta y nueve? ¡Qué antiguo!

—Oye, Carmen, ¿corres mucho? ¿Siempre haces tanto ejercicio?

—Sí, mamá y yo hacemos mucho ejercicio. Ella hace aeróbicas —así— y yo también. Hago aeróbicas todas las mañanas con mi mamá. Tenemos un video para la televisión.

—Ah... eso es bueno para los pulmones.

—Sí y para el corazón también.

—Bueno, ¿tienen ganas de ir a otra parte?

—Ay, no. Estoy cansado. Ya fuimos a la Fortaleza, al centro de viejo San Juan y ahora mismo estamos en el Morro.

—¿Ya fueron a la Plaza de Hostos?

—¿La Plaza de Hostos? Ay, no, no. ¡Carmen, si son las tres menos cinco! ¡Mamá nos espera en la Plaza de Hostos a las tres!

—¡Ay, Benjamín! Tenemos que ir rápido.

—Bueno, vamos, yo voy con ustedes, así llegan más rápido.

—¡Vamos! ¡Ándale!

Un recorrido por San Juan (a continuación)

—Pues, ¿dónde está? No la veo.

—Yo no la veo tampoco. Ay, Ben, mamá va a estar muy preocupada.

—Sí, lo sé, pero no la veo. Tal vez tenemos suerte y todavía no está aquí.

—¡Uf! Tengo sed. ¿Por qué no compramos una batida?

—¿Carmen? ¿Tienes sed? ¿Quieres una batida?

—¡Sí! Gracias.

—Vamos.

—Hola, buenas tardes.

—Hola.

—Una batida de piña, por favor.

—¿Qué es guanábana?

—Es una fruta tropical muy rica.

—Ésta es una guanábana. ¿Quieres una batida de guanábana?

—Sí, gracias. ¡Una batida de guanabána para mí!

—No, no. gua-ná-ba-na.

—Gua-ná-ba-na.

—¿Y guineo?

—Esto es un guineo.

—Ah, sí. Bueno, una batida de guineo, por favor. Pedro, yo te invito.

—¿Seguro?

—Sí.

—Muchas gracias.

—¿Cuánto es?

—Son seis dólares.

—Gracias.

—Gracias.

—Adiós.

—¿Cómo es Nueva York? ¿Te gusta vivir allí?

—Sí. Me gusta mucho mi barrio. Casi todo el mundo habla inglés y español.

—Aquí también. Oye, ¿vives en un rascacielos?

—¿Rascacielo? Por favor. No. Yo vivo en un edificio de apartamentos, pero no es un rascacielos. ¿Y a ti te gusta vivir aquí?

—No está mal.

—¿No está mal? Vives en una isla tropical.

—Sí, pero como tú, voy todos los días a la escuela, y hago mi tarea, y tengo que ayudar en la casa. Es una vida normal, como tu vida.

—Oye, Pedro, si me das tu dirección te mando una tarjeta postal de Nueva York. ¿Quieres?

—Claro que sí.

—Y yo te doy mi dirección.

—Perfecto.

—Gua-ná-ba-na. Gua-ná-ba-na. Me gusta la guanábana. Todo. ¡Me lo tomé todo! Y me gustó muchísimo.

—Carmen, ya tomaste todo el batido. Carmen, ahora vas a tener un dolor de estómago.

—Hmm... pues no me duele el estómago.

—Ay, qué linda.

Capítulo 11 *cont.*

—Ay, hijos. ¡Perdónenme! ¿Esperaron mucho
tiempo?

—No, no.

—El tráfico fue horrible.

—No, todo está bien. No te preocupes, mamá.
Mamá, él es Pedro Méndez. Mira. Él nos enseñó
el Castillo del Morro. Es de aquí, de San Juan.

—Mucho gusto.

—Pedro Méndez. Pedro Méndez. ¿Tu apellido
completo, cuál es?

—Méndez Acevedo.

—¿Méndez Acevedo?

—¿Cómo se llama tu papá?

—Se llama Ricardo.

—¿Ricardo Méndez? Y tu papá, ¿tiene un hermano
que se llama Juan?

—¡Sí! Mi tío se llama Juan.

—¡Mira! ¡Mi hermana es la esposa de tu tío Juan!

—Qué increíble, Pedro. ¡Qué casualidad! Vengan,
vamos a hablar un rato.

—Sí, vamos.

—¿Cómo está tu mamá?

—Se encuentra bien.

—Bueno, hijos, tenemos que ir. El partido de béisbol de tío Juan comienza muy pronto. Sí. Bueno,
Pedro, tú vas con tu padre, ¿verdad?

—Sí, él me espera en casa.

—Ah... muy bien. Entonces nos vemos ahí, ¿eh?
¡Carmen! Vamos.

—Hasta luego, primo.

—Hasta luego.

—Adiós.

—Oye, abuelo, y entonces fuimos al Castillo del
Morro y caminamos muchísimo. El Castillo nos
gustó mucho. ¿Verdad, Carmen?

—¡Sí! Y luego regresamos a la plaza. Y allí compramos unos batidos de fruta. Yo compré una
batida de guanábana. Y me encantó.

—Pero, ¡qué casualidad! Conocer a un primo así.
El mundo es un pañuelo, ¿verdad?

—Sí, cuando Pedro me contó lo que pasó, casi no
lo creí.

—Bueno, tal vez pueden ir ustedes a Nueva York a
visitarnos. Pedro, ¿te gustaría ir a Nueva York?

—¡Sí! ¡Muchísimo!

—Pues, tal vez el año que viene, ¿sí?

—¡Jonrón!

—¡Bravo! ¡Bravo! ¡Juan, Juan!

Panorama cultural

Although some sports, like soccer or baseball, are
perceived to be more popular in Spanish-speaking
countries, there are other sports that many people
play. In this chapter, we asked some people what
sport they play and why.

¿Qué deporte practicas?

[Víctor] Bueno, yo practico la charrería. Es el deporte nacional, el deporte mexicano. Bueno, es
este... como suertes a caballos. Es, digamos, como
en Estados Unidos los "cowboys", aquí son los,
los charros. En primer lugar mi abuelo fue charro,
y mi padre fue charro y pues... por seguir la tradición.

[Manoli] Pues practico piragüismo. Pues esto es
un K-1 (ca-uno), vamos, es... en inglés, "kayac",
por eso le decimos K-1 nosotros. Es individual nada más, o sea.. Esto es la pala. Me gusta porque el
agua me encanta, y me gusta estar aquí, vamos,
en el río.

[Raquel] Me gusta el voleibol. Es bonito jugarlo,
es un deporte, no es... es muy femenino, no es tan
masculino como el sóftbol o el fútbol soccer.

[Federico] Hago surf únicamente y juego al fútbol
con mis amigos de vez en cuando. Por qué lo hago
desde chico. Me enganché y bueno, y ahora ya no
lo puedo dejar porque no tiene comparación con
nada.

[Paula] El baloncesto y el tenis, pues son deportes que se juegan, bueno, el baloncesto en
grupo, para estar con las amigas, y el tenis para...
pues lo mismo.

[José Antonio] Practico artes marciales porque
me ayuda a conocerme a mí mismo y a prepararme
para defenderme de todas las adversidades que me
pueda traer la vida.

[Shermine] Normalmente vengo aquí al parque
del Este a practicar el voleibol desde las ocho de la
mañana hasta las 2 de la tarde. Mira, este... el
voleibol es como una fuente para desahogarse,
para, aparte para pasar tu tiempo libre, para desa-
hogar todo lo que tú has hecho en la semana, todos tus ratos amargos los dejas ahí en la cancha.

[Rodrigo] El deporte favorito mío es el futból
porque uno se fortalece los músculos y además
uno aprende.

[Javier] Pues... patinar, eh... me gusta la bicicleta,
montar en bici, me gusta también un poquito el
surf. Ah, ¿por qué? Uf, porque me la paso muy
bien patinando.

[Jenny] Bueno, patinar es lo único que me gusta
hacer. Me fascina. Es lo único en que yo puedo de-
sahogarme, divertirme, además no gasto. Ya el
único gasto que hice fue en mis patines y ya no
voy a gastar en más nada. Y es la única diversión
así, bueno, con que uno puede a la vez sudar y
hacer deporte.

[Raúl] Juego el baloncesto porque soy alto y
puedo ganar a los demás.

Videoclips

[Happydent]
Chicle Happydent sin azúcar. Hace feliz a casi todo
el mundo.

CAPÍTULO 12
Las vacaciones ideales

De antemano
Unas vacaciones ideales

—Aquí las playas son muy bonitas. Ahora mismo
estamos todos en una playa de San Juan.
Carmen está jugando con el abuelo en la arena.
Es muy tranquilo.

—¡Benjamín! Mira mi castillo.

—Sí, Carmen, ¡es tremendo!
Mamá está leyendo una novela. El jueves
fuimos al interior de Puerto Rico, al campo. Es
muy rural. Me gustó mucho.

—Papá, ¿me das el bloqueador, por favor?

—Sí, cómo no. Aquí está.

—Ay, gracias.

—¡Ay! ¡Carmen! Cuidado con las gafas de sol.

—Y el sábado... pues, el sábado fue un día maravilloso. Fuimos a un lugar muy especial.
Fuimos a un bosque tropical, El Yunque. Todo
comenzó por la mañana.

—¿Qué hacen aquí en la casa? Hoy es un día
fabuloso. Hace mucho sol. ¿Por qué no juegan
afuera? ¿Por qué no dan un paseo?

—Ay, abuelo. Carmen y yo dimos un paseo
anoche.

—Bueno, entonces... ¿por qué no visitan a los vecinos?

—Yo visité a los vecinos ayer y no hay nada interesante que hacer, abuelo.

—¿Cómo que no hay nada interesante que hacer?
Están en una isla. Hace un tiempo maravilloso y
están de vacaciones. Díganme entonces. ¿Qué
les gustaría hacer? En su opinión, ¿qué son las
vacaciones ideales?

—Hmm... ¿Las vacaciones ideales? Hmm... Ah,
¡yo sé! A mí me gustaría viajar a una selva y
bajar el río en canoa. Benjamín Corredor, explo-
rador de la selva amazónica. Me gustaría acam-
par en la selva, pescar y explorar. Sí, algún día,
espero explorar todo el río Amazonas.

—A mí me gustaría ir de vela, navegar por el
océano Pacífico en un barco de vela antiguo.
¡Pienso descubrir una isla desierta! Sí. Carmen
Corredor, marinera extraordinaria.

—¿Y qué pasa aquí? ¿De qué hablan?

—Los muchachos están aburridos.

—¿Aburridos en una isla tropical? Puerto Rico es
una maravilla y hoy, vamos a hacer un pequeño
viaje.

—¿Un viaje? ¿Adónde vamos?

—¿Y qué hacemos?

—Ya verán, ya verán. Es una sorpresa.

Unas vacaciones ideales
(a continuación)

—¿Tenemos que hacer maletas?

—No, no tenemos que hacer maletas. Pero tenemos que llevar algunas cosas.

—¿Qué cosas?

—Pues... cámara, zapatos para caminar, impermeables...

—¿Impermeables?

—Sí, impermeables, pero no se preocupen. Vayan.
Necesitan sus mochilas.

—¿Seguro que no quiere ir con nosotros?

—Sí, hija. Esta tarde pienso ir a visitar a Julio. Vamos a jugar un rato al dominó. Ayer ganó Julio.
Hoy ¡yo espero ganar!

—Aquí estamos y tenemos las mochilas.

—Bueno, papá, nos vemos esta noche.

—Bien, hija.

—Hasta entonces.

—Adiós, abuelo.

—Adiós y que se diviertan.

—Adiós, abuelo y hasta luego.

—Hasta luego.

—Pero mamá, ¿adónde vamos?

—El Yunque es un bosque tropical. Recibe más de
240 pulgadas de lluvia cada año. Es un verdadero tesoro de Puerto Rico y de todo el mundo.

—Aquí estamos en El Yunque. Vamos, hijos.
¿Quieren explorar un poco?

—¡Sí!

—¡Oye, Carmen! Ésta es una verdadera aventura.
¡Explorar en un bosque tropical, ah!

—Sí.

—¡Vamos! ¡Hay mucho que ver!

—Aquí en El Yunque viven muchísimos animales
diferentes. Realmente no hay animales peli-
grosos, pero sí hay animales en peligro de extin-
ción. Por ejemplo, hay un pájaro llamado la
cotorra, que es nativo de Puerto Rico. También
hay serpientes.

—Saben, hijos, aquí en el Yunque hay una boa
que mide hasta doce pies de largo.

—¡Doce pies de largo!

—Ajá...

—¡Qué grande! Me gustaría mucho verla.

Capítulo 12 *cont.*

—Carmencita, no vas a ver la boa. Creo que es un animal que prefiere estar muy lejos de las personas.

—En el camino encontré una orquídea. ¡Qué suerte! Era muy bonita de color violeta y blanco y muy delicada. En El Yunque las orquídeas tienen el clima perfecto para crecer. También fuimos a la Catarata de la Coca. Es una catarata maravillosa. Nos gustó muchísimo.

—Mamá me duelen los pies. Estoy cansada.

—Sí, Carmen. Caminar es buen ejercicio, pero pronto llegamos al coche. Tenemos que regresar a casa. Mañana es otro día y vamos para la playa.

—¡Para la playa! ¡Uy!

—Oye, ¿qué es eso?

—¿Qué cosa?

—Escuchen... Ese sonido, ¿qué es?

—Ah... ese sonido es el coquí. Bueno, hijos, vamos.

—El coquí es otro animal nativo de Puerto Rico. Es una rana muy, muy pequeña y sólo vive aquí en Puerto Rico. Cada tarde, cuando baja el sol, los coquíes comienzan a cantar. Caminamos mucho en El Yunque. Es muy grande y por eso sólo exploramos un poco y hay mucho más que hacer aquí en Puerto Rico. Me gustaría regresar el próximo año para ver más. Puerto Rico es un lugar ideal para pasar las vacaciones.

—¿Qué estás haciendo, Ben?

—Estoy escribiendo en mi diario. Pienso escribir sobre todas las cosas que hacemos y vemos aquí en Puerto Rico. Y pienso poner fotografías también. Mira. Aquí voy a poner la foto de nosotros delante de la Catarata y aquí espero poner una foto o una tarjeta postal de un coquí.

—¿Así que les gustó El Yunque?

—Sí, abuelo, ¡muchísimo!

—Sí, sí... increíble, abuelo.

—Díganme. ¿Todavía están aburridos?

—¡No!

Panorama cultural

If you lived in a Spanish-speaking country, what would you look forward to doing on your vacation? The answer would depend on where you lived. We asked these teenagers in Spanish-speaking countries what they do and where they go during their vacations.

¿Adónde vas y qué haces en las vacaciones?

[Camila] Voy con mi familia a Pinamar y a Uruguay a veces. Y estamos en la playa y recorremos un poco el lugar.

[Jaharlyn] Me dan dos meses en verano y tres semanas en Navidad. Lo más que hago es que voy a la playa, al río, veo televisión y duermo mucho.

[José Luis] Generalmente también voy para la playa, Puerto Cabello. Puede ser desde un mes hasta los dos meses completos de vacaciones de agosto. Con toda mi familia.

[Jennifer] En mis últimas vacaciones me fui a Chile con un grupo de amigos. Después me fui a Mar del Plata con mi familia y después me fui a pasar una semana en la casa de mi novio a Punta del Este.

[Santiago] Eh... ir a la playa y montar en bicicleta con un amigo mío.

[Luis Alfonso] Este... a veces voy, este, a la finca de mi abuela que queda allá, con mi papá, voy con, allá en San Carlos. Me quedo más o menos como una semana, y allá este, ando con mis familiares. Ando así, en bicicleta, así, en caballo.

[Magaly] Bueno, nosotros nos vamos a la playa, vamos este... a haciendas, nos divertimos.

[Jaime] Casi siempre a la playa o a la montaña. Casi siempre me gusta mejor ir a la montaña porque eh... me gusta más el frío y... escalar montes, y los animales y cosas de ese estilo.

[Shermine] Bueno, normalmente venimos nuestro equipo de voleibol aquí a practicar y a hacer eventos deportivos, que es lo que más nos motiva. Ir a la playa, me gusta bastante, y jugar mucho béisbol.

Videoclips

Y si hablamos de vacaciones no podemos dejar de mencionar el agua. La evolución de los parques acuáticos en España ha sido realmente espectacular en los últimos años. El primero en instalarse en este país lo hizo en 1984, nueve años después que apareciera el primero en California, Estados Unidos. Los parques acuáticos en España han pasado de ser pequeñas instalaciones en las playas a convertirse en grandes complejos deportivos orientados a las actividades más diversas. En ellos cada persona, según sus aficiones, puede hallar una forma de divertirse. Así podemos encontrar piscinas con escaleras colgantes, anillas desde que lanzarse, tubos deslizantes o las controladas por ordenadores, ríos rápidos con cascadas, cuevas, toboganes y un sinfín de juegos con agua que incorporan cada vez más variantes. Se calcula que en todo el mundo existen actualmente unos 300 parques acuáticos y España cuenta con un 10% de ellos, visitando sus instalaciones anualmente unas cuatro millones de personas. Una de las mejores zonas de Europa para un parque es justamente el litoral mediterráneo español. El alto número de días calurosos y los millones de turistas que visitan su territorio anualmente son garantías de éxito muy importantes para los impresarios que han decidido invertir en este nuevo tipo de parque de atracciones al aire libre.

Answer Key

Preliminary Chapter Activity Master 1

1. 1. b
   2. c
   3. a
   4. d
2. 3
   8
   10
   1
   5
   7
   2
   9
   6
   4
   11
3. Africa, Europe, North America, South America, Asia

Location Opener 1 Activity Master

1. All items should be checked.
2. 1. e
   2. c
   3. a
   4. d
   5. b
3. 1. b
   2. d
   3. a
   4. c

Chapter 1 Activity Master 1

1. Answers will vary.
2. 1. c
   2. b
   3. d
   4. a
3. 1. c
   2. a
   3. b
   4. d
4. c

Chapter 1 Activity Master 2

1. a, c, f
2. Mercedes
3. Francisco
4. sincero, inteligente, organizado, alto y muy guapo
5. Answers will vary.

Chapter 1 Activity Master 3

1. Ivette—Puerto Rico
   Sandra—Venezuela
   Mauricio—Costa Rica
   Miguel—España
2. 1. c
   2. a
   3. d
   4. e
   5. b
3. 4
4. Answers will vary.

Chapter 2 Activity Master 1

1. 1, 2, 3, 6
2. 1. A
   2. P
   3. A
   4. A
   5. P
3. a. necesita
   b. no necesita
   c. no necesita
   d. quiere
   e. quiere
   f. necesita

Chapter 2 Activity Master 2

1. a, b
2. un cuaderno rojo, dos cuadernos rojos, un cuaderno amarillo, un cuaderno verde
3. 4, 3, 1, 2, 5
4. Answers will vary.

Chapter 2 Activity Master 3

1. a. F
   b. P, J, F
   c. J
   d. J, F
   e. J
   f. J
   g. P, F
   h. P
   i. F
   j. J
   k. J
   l. J
2. 1. a, b
   2. c, d
   3. c
   4. a
3. Answers will vary.
4. Answers will vary.

Location Opener 2 Activity Master

1. 1, 3, 4
2. 1. C
   2. F
   3. F
   4. C
   5. C
3. 1. c
   2. b
   3. a

Chapter 3 Activity Master 1

1. 1, 2, 4
2. 1. b
   2. c
   3. a
   4. d
3. 1. b
   2. d
   3. a
   4. c

Chapter 3 Activity Master 2

1. Answers will vary.
2. 1. d
   2. a
   3. b
   4. c
3. 1. F
   2. F
   3. C
   4. C
   5. F

Chapter 3 Activity Master 3

1. MARIO: 7, 12:30
   NATALIE: 7; 1:30; 3
2. GALA: 12:30
   JUAN: 8:00
   LUCILA: 12:15
3. a, b, d
4. 20; 10; 7; 2

Chapter 4 Activity Master 1

1. Answers will vary.
2. a, b, c, e, g
3. a. 6
   b. 2
   c. 1
   d. 3
   e. 4
   f. 5

Chapter 4 Activity Master 2

1. CLAUDIA: e; c; d
   LUIS: a
   CLAUDIA: b
2. a, b, e, g
3. 1. F
   2. C
   3. F
   4. C

Chapter 4 Activity Master 3

1. 1. c
   2. a
   3. d
   4. b
2. a. C
   b. F
   c. C
   d. C
   e. C
   f. F
   g. C
   h. F
3. b: A David le gusta pasear con sus amigos.
   f: Para Leslie el paseo es divertido.
   h: Kevin va a la playa.
4. b, c

Location Opener 3 Activity Master

1. a, b, d, f
2. **a.** C
   b. F; La mayoría de los hispanoha-blantes en la Florida son cubanos.
   c. F; Hay tiendas y restaurantes.
   d. C
   e. C
3. estados
   clima
   playas
   cosmopolita

Chapter 5 Activity Master 1

1. 1. edition
   2. program
   3. temperature
   4. report
   5. activities
   6. camera
2. 1. c
   2. e
   3. d
   4. a
   5. b
3. 1. a, b
   2. a, b
   3. b
   4. a, b
4. 1. Panamá
   2. Tamayo
   3. pintar/dibujar
   4. dibujar/pintar

Chapter 5 Activity Master 2

1. Club de ecología; Club de ciencias
2. 1. c
   2. d
   3. a
   4. b
   5. e
3. 1. c
   2. f
   3. d
   4. b
   5. a
   6. e
4. Answers will vary.

Chapter 5 Activity Master 3

1. a, c, d, e, h, i
2. Lucía: tocar la guitarra; mirar televisión
   Marcelo: mirar televisión
   Güido: mirar televisión; trabajar; hacer tarea
   Jesús: hacer tarea; ir al Ávila
   Juan Fernando: hacer tarea
3. Maikel, Güido, Jesús, Juan Fernando
4. 1. no
   2. sí
   3. no
   4. sí
   5. sí

Chapter 6 Activity Master 1

1. Answers will vary.
2. 1. a
   2. b
   3. c
   4. b
   5. b
3. 1. b, c, f
   2. a, c, d
   3. b, c, e
4. Answers will vary.

Chapter 6 Activity Master 2

1. Answers will vary.
2. **a.** 3
   b. 5
   c. 2
   d. 4
   e. 1
3. 1. cariñoso
   2. tres
   3. jugar
   4. travieso
   5. azul
4. Answers will vary.

Chapter 6 Activity Master 3

1. 1. b
   2. c
   3. e
   4. a
   5. d

2. **a.** 5
   b. 5
   c. 5
   d. 7
   e. 4
   f. 5
   g. 4
3. Arantxa: vacuum, sweep
   Éric: sweep
   Angie: cook
   Paola: cook, wash dishes, sweep
4. bueno; familia; es; vivir

Location Opener 4 Activity Master

1. a, b, c, e, f, g, i, j
2. 1. d
   2. c
   3. b
   4. a
3. Possible answer: Los habitantes de Otavalo son famosos por sus textiles.

Chapter 7 Activity Master 1

1. b, c, a
2. 1. c
   2. a
   3. b
   4. d
3. 1. F
   2. F
   3. C
   4. C
   5. C
4. a

Chapter 7 Activity Master 2

1. c
2. 1. b
   2. c
   3. a
3. es estudiante; es de San Francisco; tiene 17 años; va a vivir en Quito
4. **a.** 3
   b. 1
   c. 5
   d. 4
   e. 2

Chapter 7 Activity Master 3

1. 1. b
   2. a
   3. c

2. 1. a
   2. c
   3. e
   4. b
   5. d
3. Rodrigo: el hombre; Jessica: el hombre; María Isabel: el hombre; Ixchel: los dos; Carlos: los dos
4. b
5. b

Chapter 8 Activity Master 1

1. 1. b, f
   2. a, f
   3. c, f
   4. d, f
2. b
3. papas: b
   cebollas: a
   aguacate: b
   chiles: a
   tomate: a
   queso: b
4. Answers will vary.
5. 1. a
   2. b
   3. b

Chapter 8 Activity Master 2

1. Answers will vary.
2. 1. b, c
   2. e, c
3. **a.** 2
   b. 5
   c. 1
   d. 3
   e. 4
4. Answers will vary.

Chapter 8 Activity Master 3

1. 1. c
   2. a
   3. b
2. 1. c
   2. e
   3. a
   4. d
   5. b
3. 1. b
   2. a
   3. c
4. 1. La Casera
   2. Leche Ram
   3. Néctares Dos Pinos

Spanish 1 ¡Ven conmigo!

Location Opener 5 Activity Master

1. a, c, d, e, f, g, j, k, l
2. d

Chapter 9 Activity Master 1

1. Answers will vary.
2. a, c, d, e, g
3. **a.** 2
   b. 3
   c. 1
4. 1. C
   2. C
   3. F
   4. F
   5. F
   6. C
5. 3. Lisa no compra la falda.
   4. Le compran un cartel.
   5. Pasan media hora en buscar algo.

Chapter 9 Activity Master 2

1. un cartel
2. 1. G
   2. G
   3. E
   4. L
   5. G
3. 1—b; 3— a , 2—c

Chapter 9 Activity Master 3

1. Answers will vary.
2. a, c, e, f
3. 3, 5
4. b, c, f

Chapter 10 Activity Master 1

1. Apellido: Villarreal; Nombre: Manuel;
   Tipo de pastel: chocolate, Mensaje:
   Felicidades en el día de tu graduación,
   Héctor
2. 1. b
   2. d
   3. a
   4. c
3. 1. a, b
   2. c
   3. b
   4. c
4. c

Chapter 10 Activity Master 2

1. 2, 3, 4
2. **a.** 3; compraron
   b. 2; llamó
   c. 4; regresaron
   d. 5; llegó
   e. 1; mandó
3. 1. El señor Villarreal no mandó las in-
      vitaciones.
   2. Las chicas compraron un pastel para
      una fiesta de quinceañera.
   3. Héctor salió del trabajo temprano.

Chapter 10 Activity Master 3

1. 1. a
   2. c
   3. b
2. 1. R
   2. H
   3. H
   4. R
   5. H
   6. H
   7. R
   8. H
3. 1. d
   2. b
   3. c
   4. a
4. a

Location Opener 6 Activity Master

1. 1. e
   2. c
   3. a
   4. d
   5. b
2. 1. isla
   2. capital
   3. playas
   4. animales
3. b

Chapter 11 Activity Master 1

1. el corazón; la nariz; los pies; los pulmones; las orejas
2. Ben: inline skating, baseball
   Carmen: aerobics; ice skating
   Pedro: ice skating; baseball
   el tío: baseball

3. 1. a
    2. c
    3. b
    4. d
4. a. 5
    b. 4
    c. 3
    d. 1
    e. 2

Chapter 11 Activity Master 2

1. They have to go to **la Plaza de Hostos** to meet their mother at 3:00.
2. 1. c
    2. b
    3. a
    4. a
3. a. 3; b. 4; c. 2; d. 1
4. 1. Carmen pide una batida de guanábana.
    2. La mamá de Carmen y Ben llega tarde a la plaza.
    3. En el barrio de Ben se habla inglés y español.
    4. Pedro va a la escuela todos los días.
    5. El tío Juan juega al béisbol en Puerto Rico.

Chapter 11 Activity Master 3

1. Víctor; la charrería; por seguir la tradición
    Manoli; el piragüismo; el agua me encanta
    Raquel; el voleibol; no es masculino
2. 1. Paula
    2. Federico
    3. Shermine
    4. Víctor
    5. Federico
    6. José Antonio
3. 1. I
    2. I
    3. E
    4. A
    5. A
    6. I
    7. E
    8. E
    9. I
    10. I
    11. E
4. 1. F
    2. F
    3. F

Chapter 12 Activity Master 1

1. a. Ben
    b. Carmen
2. 1. F
    2. F
    3. C
    4. C
3. 1. Ben
    2. explorar
    3. playa
    4. San Juan
    5. novela
    6. vecinos
       selva

Chapter 12 Activity Master 2

1. Answers will vary.
2. 1, 5, 7
3. 1. F
    2. C
    3. F
    4. C
    5. F
4. 1. c. La mamá de Ben y Carmen tiene una sorpresa para ellos.
    2. b. Ben, Carmen y su mamá van a El Yunque.
    3. a. Después van a la playa.

Chapter 12 Activity Master 3

1. Camila: ir a Uruguay; ir a la playa
    Jaharlyn: ver televisión; dormir mucho; ir a la playa
    José Luis: ir a la playa
2. 1, 2, 3, 4, 5, 7, 8
3. 1. a
    2. d
    3. b
    4. c
4. 1–piscinas con escaleras colgantes; 2–anillas; 3–tubos deslizantes; 4–ríos rápidos con cascadas; 5–toboganes
5. 300; 10; 4

Spanish 1 ¡Ven conmigo!